THE
OMNIPRESENT
I AM,
EVIDENCED

Volume Two

Writings by the Author

The Ultimate
Prayers and Excerpts from The Word
Success Is Normal, Just Be Yourself,
 Your Eternal Identity
Fulfillment of Purpose, Volume One
Fulfillment of Purpose, Volume Two
You Are the Splendor
Gems & Poems of The Ultimate
The Gospel According to Thomas
Three Essential Steps
The Omnipresent I AM, Volume One
The Omnipresent I AM, Evidenced, Volume Two
The Ultimate Awareness, an Eternal Constant,
 Volume One
The Ultimate Awareness, an Eternal Constant,
 Volume Two

These and other books available through:
Mystics of the World
Eliot, Maine
www.mysticsoftheworld.com

THE
OMNIPRESENT
I AM,
EVIDENCED

Volume Two

Marie S. Watts

The Omnipresent I AM, Evidenced
Volume Two
by Marie S. Watts

Mystics of the World First Edition 2015   1967
Published by Mystics of the World
ISBN-13: 978-0692603468 (Mystics of the World)
ISBN-10: 0692603468

For information contact:
Mystics of the World
Eliot, Maine
www.mysticsoftheworld.com

Photography by © Dr. Joel Murphy 2015
www.DrJMphotography.zenfolio.com
Printed by CreateSpace
Available from Mystics of the World and Amazon.com

Contents

Introduction

This, the second of two volumes of classwork, represents the evening sessions of the gloriously enlightened class experienced in 1966, in Vista, California and in New York City. The revelations of the morning sessions are contained in Volume One of this work. Those of you who attended these class sessions know the glorious Light we experienced. And most wonderful of all is the fact that this class experience is continuing daily and hourly in and as the experience of all of us.

The purpose of this presentation of our class is two-fold. First, it is intended to be an ever available record and reminder of the omnipresent, omnipotent, eternal, constant *I* that You are, and to present those revelations which have been experienced since the close of the class sessions. Second, it is the purpose of the Love we are, to make these revelations available to those students who were prepared for them but were unable to attend the class sessions.

In this second volume of classwork, you will discover how it is, and why it is, that you are eternal, constant, universal Perfection. You will perceive the true Nature and Activity of the atom. You will realize, more than ever before, the infinite, indivisible Nature of the Substance of all Form.

It is my hope that you have studied and contemplated the first volume of this work. The morning sessions, as presented in Volume One, are a complete presentation of the universal, omnipresent, omnipotent, omniactive *I* that You are. And the evening sessions, as presented in this volume, are a complete presentation of the way in which this infinite *I*, in ceaseless action, is evidenced in and as your daily experience, your Supply, and your Body. Indeed, the morning and evening sessions combined are a gloriously complete revelation of the forever fact that God *is* All, All *is* God, and that this "isness" is what you are and all that it is possible for you to be.

Indeed, it is necessary for you to *know* the Truth. It is essential to have and to *be* full knowledge of all that is true, genuine, actual, real. Knowledge is power. This is true because the conscious, living Mind that knows the Truth *is* the Substance and the Activity of the Truth It knows and knows Itself to be.

Beloved, the Truths revealed in the two volumes of this classwork do present the knowledge that is power. Knowing the power and the glory of these Truths and knowing that *You* are every Truth herein revealed, I lovingly dedicate this second volume of classwork to You, the Reader.

Boundless Light and Love,
Marie S. Watts

Chapter I

The Omnipresent I AM, Evidenced

There is no fear in love; but perfect love casteth out fear: because fear hath torment. He that feareth is not made perfect in love.

—I John 4:18

God is Love. Love is God. If there were no God, there would be no Love. If there were no Love, there would be no God. The word *God* means Love to those of us who consciously experience *being* the Love that is God. Whenever we hear, speak, read, or write the word *God*, we are aware of the Omnipresence which is Love. In like manner, the word *Love* always signifies to us the Omnipresence which is God.

Truly, there is no fear when we are conscious of the forever fact that Love is All, All is Love, even as God is All, All is God. In our perception of this Truth, we are conscious of being the one and only Mind, to whom fear is unknown. It is utterly impossible to simultaneously experience being Love and to experience fear. The constant, surging, flowing Presence of Love Itself precludes the possibility of fear or of anything to fear.

There really is but one Mind, and this Mind is completely unaware of fear. The necessity is to perceive that neither fear *nor a mind that can know fear* exists. The illusion that is called fear is ignorance. It is not ignorance from the standpoint of stupidity. Rather, it is a seeming lack, or absence, of knowledge of the genuine and *only* Substance and Activity which is eternal Perfection in action.

The first reaction of primitive man to anything he did not understand was fear. This assumptive man did not understand the sun, moon, or stars. Neither did he have knowledge of the elements such as the wind, the waves, rain, thunder, or lightning. This apparent ignorance seemed to arouse great fear. Such ignorance and fear gave these perfectly natural existents the only destructive power they even *seemed* to have. This apparent destructive power was never in the sun, moon, or stars. Neither was it the wind, rain, thunder, or lightning. Rather, it was assumptive man's illusory fear of that which he did not know or understand that attached the power of destruction to the sun, moon, stars, and the elements.

Throughout the ages this delusion—fear of the unknown—has continued, and is continuing, right today. So-called man, apparently being without knowledge of that which is true, of *that which really is Existence*—continues to fear the winds, the waves, the elements; thus, they can seem to be dangerous or destructive. But this is not all; this same illusion of fear pertains to anything about which man is ignorant or that he does not understand. Do you know that there are some sincere students of Truth who are actually afraid of the Absolute Truth? Thus, this seeming fear acts as a deterrent to their revelation. They dare not go all the way in their perception of the glorious Truth that God really is All, All really is God. It is this same illusion of fear that seems to be rampant where the Body is concerned. You see, this Body right here is not the way It appears to be, and all fear for the Body is predicated in ignorance—lack of knowledge—of the constant, eternal, perfect, and immutable Substance in Form that is this Body. Today assumptive man seems to be tormented by fear of an ever increasing number and variety of diseases. Admittedly, the medical profession has made tremendous strides in the treatment of these seeming imperfections, and they are constantly seeking for new "cures" for those diseases that are supposedly incurable. Despite this fact, frequently there are reports of some hitherto unknown disease, and then the search begins for a new cure for the new disease.

It does appear that this seemingly mortal existence is a constant treadmill of one illusory illness after another, and man constantly appears to become more fearful. Here is a very important fact that we should realize right now:

The seeming disease and the mind that fears the disease are one and the same thing, and this is sheer illusion, without an iota of genuineness or truth at all.

Nonetheless, so long as this illusory fear and ignorance continue to claim to be the mind of man, illness, pain, age, and death will also continue to be the lot of so-called man.

When *knowledge* of the genuine Nature of Body is present, there can never be any fear for, or concern about, this glorious, perfect, eternal Body. As stated before, fear and ignorance of that which is true do seem to portray themselves as illness and as a temporary, perishable body. But by this same token, knowledge of just what constitutes the Substance and the Activity of this Body completely dispels all ignorance about it. Thus, the All-knowing Mind—all Knowledge—is completely free from fear, concern, discouragement, or ignorance.

Whatever assumptive man appears to fear will always seem to have power to harm or to destroy him. But actually, the only power that so-called evil even *seems* to have is man's apparent fear of it and his belief in it. This is why it is of the utmost importance for us to really know the true Substance that is this Body. It is essential that we have complete knowledge of the constant, eternal, changeless Nature of this Substance in Form. But above all, we must know why this Body is eternal, indestructible, and forever imperishable. And our "knowing" would not be complete unless we were aware of the ceaseless, perfect, rhythmic activity of this Substance in Form.

Chapter II

Substance Is Perfection

Let us now perceive the genuine and only Nature of all Substance in Form—and all Substance *is* in Form. Let us further perceive how it is, and why it is, that all Substance is immutable, imperishable, indestructible, and eternal. This is the knowledge that is so necessary if we are to transcend all so-called ignorance and the fear that always seems to accompany this illusory ignorance, You see, it is through this omnipotent knowledge that we realize complete freedom from all fear, uncertainty, and frustration. In order that this freedom be completely perceived and manifested, it is important that we perceive the significant fact that we *are* the entire Truth, the sum total of all that is true and of nothing else, for there is nothing else for us to be.

Perfection is an Absolute Truth. The word *Absolute* means complete Perfection. Actually, every Truth is an Absolute Truth. Every Truth is a universal Truth. This means that every Truth is present, and *equally* present, everywhere.

Truthfully, it could be said that Perfection is that omnipresent aspect of Truth that is Principle. It is impossible to imagine Principle as being imperfect. And obviously, Principle is everywhere present, and everywhere equally present. Well, this perfect, eternal, omnipresent Principle *is* Perfection.

Perfection is a universal, eternal Constant; thus, there can never be a beginning, nor can there be an ending to this universally constant Truth — Perfection. Being an omnipresent, eternal, universal Constant, never can there be an interruption of the constancy which is Perfection. There is not, never has been, nor will there ever be anything that is perfect today and imperfect tomorrow. Neither can anything that appeared to be imperfect yesterday become perfect tomorrow because, as we stated before, Perfection is an eternal Constant.

Perfection without Its manifestation of Itself would be purposeless, and such an impossibility would mean an absence of Mind, Intelligence. Furthermore, Absolute Perfection can *only* manifest Itself as what It is — Perfection. The manifestation of Perfection has to be as completely perfect as is the Principle — Perfection — Itself.

This is true because the manifestation of Perfection is the very presence of the Principle — Perfection. Hence, any *seeming* manifestation of imperfection is completely false and illusory, for there simply is no imperfection to be manifested. Perfection being a universal, constant Principle, there is not one split second in which imperfection can be manifested. Its constant Presence cannot be interrupted, nor can It be absent. Because Perfection is an omnipresent Existent, there is not a pinpoint of

Infinity in which It does not exist. Never can there be an absence of Perfection. Nowhere can there be an absence of Perfection. This is why any seeming manifestation of imperfection is utterly and completely false.

To fear the absence of something that is always present is ludicrous. This is true, even though that which is present may seem to be temporarily concealed. For instance, even though clouds may occasionally obscure the sun, it would never occur to us to imagine that the sun was absent. Neither would we believe or fear the absence of the ever-present sun. Yet when it appears that ever-present Perfection is obscured or concealed, we do tend to consider this omnipresent Existent to be absent, and sometimes we even fear that It is permanently absent.

To fear an absence of Perfection, which is always present, is only an apparent lack of knowledge of that which is present. Consequently, the very instant that we know—really know—that Perfection is all that is present, we experience the evidence of this Truth that we know.

Again, let us state:

The conscious, living Mind that *knows* any Truth—anything that is true or a fact—*is* the very Substance, Form, and Activity of that Truth which It knows.

Mind really is Substance. Consciousness really is Substance. All Substance is a living Substance, so Life is Substance. Thus, conscious, living Mind, constantly knowing just what It is, is conscious of *being* perfect Substance.

Chapter III

The Atom

Now that we are discussing the word *Substance*, let us consider the word *atom* for a few moments. We have been told that an atom is an infinitesimal piece of matter. Then, conversely, the physicists are arriving at the conclusion that matter, as such, does not exist. Some of them frankly state that matter as we see it is sheer illusion. Nonetheless, there is something here which has been given the name "atom." This is a fact, in the same way that there is something here that is given the name "body."

Now, let us perceive just what an atom really is. We have said that we were going to be specific in this class experience, and the consideration of the atom is just about as specific as it is possible for us to be.

The physicists now tell us that, in appearance, the atom may be compared to our solar system. Now, we have discussed the atom in former classes, and we will not repeat the identical statements which have already been presented. Yet because our enlightenment is now apparently greater, we must make a few statements that are similar to previous statements. These are a basis, or foundation, for that which is to follow. It is of the utmost importance that we really *know* completely the nature of all the substance and activity of the atom. This is true because the entire Substance that is this boundless Universe consists of what the physicists call atoms. Thus, it naturally follows that the Substance in Form called this Body, right here and now, has to consist of what is called atoms. We must continue on and on until we really know and experience *being* the ever perfect, indestructible, imperishable, eternal Body.

We have stated that it is now believed by the physicists that the structure, the substance, and the activity of the atom may be compared to the Nature and Activity of our solar system. Of course this is true because the nature and activity of the atom is identically the same as is the Nature of our solar system. Furthermore, the activity of the atom is identically the same as is the Activity of our solar system. If these statements seem a bit far-fetched, please bear with us. All of this will be clarified as we continue. It is necessary to make these statements right now in order to clearly present the following revelations of Body and Its Activity.

Let us repeat: the nature and activity of the atom is identically the same as is the Nature of our solar system. Do you see what this means? It means that this Body, which is said to be comprised of innumerable atoms, really consists of the very same Substance and Activity that exists as this solar system, this galaxy, and the entire, boundless Universe Itself.

As one of the students of the Ultimate stated so succinctly, "We are going to have to exchange the Adam myth for the atom fact." And the atom fact is the eternal, perfect Substance and Activity which comprises *all* Substance in Form.

In the course of our consideration of the atom, we are going to perceive that it is not a destructive Substance at all. Rather, our clear perception of the genuine Nature of the atom will reveal how it is, and why it is, that all Substance in Form is eternal, perfect, indestructible, and imperishable. How could it be otherwise, when all Substance consists of atoms and the atom is eternal, indestructible, and imperishable? As we "exchange the Adam myth for the atom fact," we will completely dispose of any illusion of a created man, and we will perceive the fact that all Substance — thus, all Substance in Form — is eternal.

It is true that some of the physicists make statements that would certainly indicate that the atom could be destroyed. Such statements as "We have split the atom" or "We smash the atom" really sound as though the atom were a destructible, perishable substance. But subsequent revelations will reveal that it is not possible to destroy the atom.

Furthermore, we are to perceive just *why* it is impossible for the atom to be destroyed or to perish. Some of the physicists do state that the atom is indestructible. So it is known that the atom is eternal and indestructible. It is also known that all Substance consists of atoms. This being true, it follows that all Substance is indestructible because all Substance consists of atoms.

Now, of course, we are not speaking about a pseudo substance called matter. *There is no matter.* That which is called matter is simply the mistaken way that so-called "man with breath in his nostrils" misperceives and misinterprets the genuine and only Substance that *is*. It is this same misconception, called man, who apparently believes that all Substance begins and must end. And, of course, this means that this assumptive man falsely believes that Life, Mind, Consciousness, Love are temporary. Nothing could be further from the Truth.

As you know, the Body is supposed to deteriorate, age, and finally disintegrate and disappear as the manifest Body. But the Body is also supposed to be created, and then in turn it is supposed to create other bodies. Once it is clearly seen that the genuine and *only* Substance of the Body is beginningless, changeless, and endless, the fantasy of a body that begins and ends will be exposed and obliterated.

This true perception of the Body, consisting of a Substance that is so enduring that It is everlasting, is here to be perceived. And it must be perceived because right now there is an absolute necessity to actually *know* the eternal Nature of the Body and why It is eternal. The horrendous appearance of the seemingly destructive elements of the atom makes it imperative that we know the genuine Nature of all

Substance. However, the perception of the eternal Body can only be complete when we know *why* this Substance in Form cannot be destroyed and *why* It cannot perish.

This knowledge necessitates a complete comprehension of that which comprises the Body — and all Substance. Of course, this means that we must really know exactly what comprises the atom and its activity because all Substance consists of atoms. Furthermore, we must perceive that matter, as such, does not exist and why there is not, and cannot be, that which is called matter.

Now we are going to perceive just why it is that matter, as such, does not exist. But we are also going to know why it is that the Substance in Form that does exist is eternal, indestructible, immutable, and imperishable. In order to understand the "why" of this Truth, it is necessary to know what the Substance of that which is called atom really is and how It acts. In short, we are going to have to know just what the basic and only Substance that is the Entirety — the boundless Universe — really is and how It fulfills Its purpose in being.

Of course, in the final analysis, we do perceive that It is all God and nothing but God. God *is* All, All *is* God. Always remember that anything, by any name, is just God referred to by that particular name or word. It makes no difference whether we speak of atoms, stars, planets, trees, or blades of grass — we know that we are speaking of God and God alone.

What is an atom? The physicists say that an atom consists of infinitesimal particles of *energy*. The nucleus at the center of the atom is also believed to consist of tiny bits of *energy*, and the nucleus is said to consist of other particles of *energy* called neutrons and protons. The particles of energy called electrons are constantly circling, or orbiting, around the *energy* called the nucleus. They move in a definite pattern, and it is said that they are controlled and held in their proper orbit by the nucleus around which they orbit.

Often we read a simile of the atom, written by a physicist, and almost invariably the atom is compared to our solar system. The nucleus at the center of the atom is compared to our sun, and the electrons, which are said to be orbiting in a perfect pattern around the nucleus, are compared to the various planets—Earth, Mars, Venus, etc.—which orbit around our sun.

Now, the atom is considered to be so infinitesimal that it has been said to be impossible to isolate just one single atom. Yet these tiny segments of energy are believed to be the entire substance of all that is called—but is not—material.

For instance, the air, all liquid, all so-called gases, the Earth, all that is supposed to be solid, such as flowers, vegetables, minerals, and the like, are said to consist of atoms. Needless to say, this means that all that is supposed to comprise the Body is considered to be atoms.

Right here, it is well to be completely clear on one aspect of the atom. The basic substance of this minute speck of *energy* remains exactly the same. This is true whether the atomic substance be called liquid, solid, gaseous, or whatever. This basic essence never changes into another kind of substance. However, there *is* distinction existing as these atoms. This distinction consists of the number of electrons orbiting around the nucleus and the pattern or design in which they orbit.

From the foregoing statements, we can perceive that the difference in the substance of the water we drink, the food we eat, the air we breathe, and *this Body right here* is the distinct number of atoms involved and the pattern in which they orbit. However, there is another distinction in the atomic substance. This distinction is in the rhythmic tempos of the revolving electrons. As we continue in our consideration of these revelations, we will discover that this paragraph and its revelations are of vital importance.

Just recently, I read an article in which there were some statements that were attributed to one of our leading physicists. In this article, the writer presents a very pertinent viewpoint of a physicist— namely, there is a basic *unity* between all the substances that comprise this Universe, and this unity rests in the essence and activity of the atom— nucleus, protons, neutrons, and electrons—which comprises all substance.

Well, this is decidedly encouraging. Yet there will come a day when all of us will clearly perceive the fact that there is more than unity *between* all Substance in Form. We will know beyond any doubt that all Substance *is* in Form and that the Form does not divide the universal Substance — God — into bits and particles of Itself. Yes, we shall realize that this boundless Universe is inseparably One and that Its Activity is as indivisible as is Its Essence. (Beloved, I must digress here for just a moment to state that this inseparable Oneness, acting in such perfection and harmony, is Love, and God is Love, even as Love is God.)

Let us now return to our consideration of the atom. You will recall that in a few previous paragraphs, the word *energy* was italicized. There was a purpose in the accentuation of this word. In fact, there is a very important purpose to be fulfilled through the true perception of that which is called energy and its activity.

Right here and now, I must make an unequivocal statement: *no atom can ever disappear or be destroyed.* This is an absolute Truth, despite the terminology that is used, such as "splitting" or "smashing" the atom. This terminology makes it *appear* that the atom can be separated or that it is subject to destruction or extinction. Nonetheless, the fact remains: the Essence of the atom is eternal. It did not come into being, nor can it depart from — or be forced out of — being. It was *never created*, nor can it be put out of existence. Why is this true? It is a fact because the atom does not consist of a kind of substance that is temporary or that is destructible.

Now, let us discover just why the atom is indestructible and eternal. The atom is indestructible and eternal because it consists of a kind of Substance that cannot begin or end; neither can it ever be destroyed. What is this eternal, indestructible Substance? It is that which the physicists call *energy*.

In order to substantiate the foregoing statements, let us once more consider, briefly, the Substance of which the atom is composed. The nucleus at the center of the atom consists of minute particles of energy called neutrons and protons. This nucleus controls the perfect pattern in which the energy called electrons revolves around the central field of energy called the nucleus. From these facts, it is obvious that the entire essence of the atom is what the physicists call *energy*.

Here we have infinitesimal particles of energy, revolving around and controlled by a central field of energy called a nucleus. Now we can determine the fact that the entire Substance of the atom is that which the physicists call *energy*.

It now becomes imperative for us to know what comprises energy. In this knowledge, there is an awareness of just why the atom is eternal and indestructible. This knowledge is vitally important because it reveals why all Substance is eternal and indestructible. Whether the Substance be in the form of a leaf, a tree, or the Body makes no difference. In order to be Substance, It has to consist of that which is called *energy*, which is eternal, thus, indestructible.

What is energy?

> Energy is Life. Light is Life; therefore, the Substance of all Form is *living* Light.

For years, most of us have read, and said, that God is all Substance. And of course, this was a statement of absolute Truth. But we were just not aware of the full import of this statement. Now we know why it is a statement of fact, or a true statement. God is Life. Life is God. Life is Light. And the Life that is Light—the Light which is Life—is the Substance of that which is called the atom—namely *energy*. This Substance in Form called the atom can no more begin or end than can God begin or end, because this Substance *is* God. It can no more be destroyed, or perish, than God can be destroyed, or perish, because It is eternal Life, God Itself.

Oh, Beloved, it is so apparent that no matter how many words we use or how materialistic they may appear to be, always we are speaking, reading, or writing of God. It is all God, for there is nothing else for It to be.

Chapter IV

The Perfect Atom in Perfect Activity

Now it becomes necessary for us to consider the ceaseless activity which is eternally present in and *as* every so-called atom.

We have perceived the fact that the boundless Universe consists of atoms. We have also compared the Substance, Form, and Activity of each atom with the Substance, Form, and Activity of our solar system. We know that the Substance which is called the nucleus at the center of the atom may be compared to our sun, and that which is called the electrons, which revolve around the nucleus, may be compared to the planets, etc., which orbit in such perfect activity around the sun.

We can now perceive the omnipresent activity and the absolute perfection of this perfect Substance in action. But we can also perceive the perfect activity of the perfect Substance—the atom, or energy.

Of course, we cannot avoid perceiving the perfect order, the perfect control, and the perfect balance of this orbital activity. We note that whether it be the perfect activity of the atom or the perfect, orderly, controlled, balanced activity of our solar system, the activity remains identical.

Let us not overlook the fact that the Substance in Form, as well as the Form Itself, consists of the very same identical Perfection, whether It be evidenced as the atom or whether It be evidenced as our solar system. It can be no other way because the boundless Universe Itself—God—consists of that which the physicists call atoms. It is of vital importance for us to clearly perceive the important fact that the Substance and Activity of the most infinitesimal so-called element, or aspect, of the atom is identically the same Substance and Activity that comprises our solar system. We shall soon be aware of greater vistas of this magnificent revelation as we continue on in our reading and contemplation.

Now, we must never omit the word *Love*. What is it that makes this Substance, Its Form, and Its Activity so gloriously perfect and eternally harmonious? It is Love, Love, Love. Oh, yes, It is all that God, Mind, Life, Consciousness is, but the *fire* of It, the inspiration, the very Power of It, is Love. It is Love that maintains the perfect order, the control, the balance of all that comprises the so-called atom, our solar system, our galaxy, every galaxy, and the entire boundless, living Universe.

Always, we must be aware of the Omnipresence that is Love. It is only in this way that we can avoid the seeming cold intellectuality which *seems* so apparent in many students. It is only in this way that we can be fully and gloriously aware of the forever fact that *we* are Love Itself. *Love is the Power of this entire Absolute Truth.*

Yes, all Substance is Perfection. All Form is Perfection. All Activity is Perfection in action. Now that we have reminded ourselves of the most important aspect of all—Love—let us observe the obvious fact that this perfect, orderly, controlled, balanced activity is *intelligent* activity. It is Mind—Intelligence—in action.

We know that Activity is Life. Without Life, there could be no Activity, even as without Activity, there could be no Life. There is nothing that lives—nothing that is alive—but Life. Hence, the only Life in existence is perfect, constant, eternal Life.

Now, we have discussed—and will frequently discuss—the word *Love.* We have also discussed *Mind,* or *Intelligence,* and the word *Life,* which is of such tremendous importance. Let us consider the great significance of the word *Consciousness.*

There is activity everywhere. It is inconceivable that there could be one iota of this boundless, living Universe wherein there was no activity. Now, in order that there be activity, there has to be something to act. There is! And this Something that acts is Consciousness—or Spirit, if you prefer this word. But Consciousness, Life, Mind, Love are inseparable. So that which is constantly active is intelligent, living, loving Consciousness. Of course, we can rearrange these words in any way without changing the significance of their spiritual meaning. For instance, we could say, "loving, living, conscious Mind" or "conscious, living, intelligent Love."

Now, because every Truth we perceive is true specifically as well as universally, let us perceive why it may be helpful to transpose these four words, should there seem to be some inharmony.

For instance, if it appears that some mental inharmony is presented, it is helpful to contemplate the word *Mind*. Perhaps some difficulty pertaining to the Substance in Form called the Body may *seem* to present a problem. In this case, it may be most enlightening to contemplate the word *Consciousness*.

Beloved, please do not consider what we are saying here as though it were a method or formula for your contemplation. Always, your contemplation must take place in the way it reveals itself as your own Consciousness.

After we have contemplated the entire Substance, Form, and Activity that is this boundless Ocean of living Light — the Universe — it does appear to be helpful to consider that aspect of our universal Being which pertains to the Truth about that which *appears* to be troublesome.

We have often read, heard, and spoken of the spiritual Body, or the Body of Spirit. Somehow, this word *Spirit* is more comprehensive when considered from the standpoint of Consciousness. Of course, even though we use these four words interchangeably, you will realize that never is there any division between Life, Mind, Love, and Consciousness. There are many words that we use in our symbology, but never do we mean, or even imply, separation of the *one infinite, inseparable All.* In this paragraph, we have only discussed certain aspects of the universal Consciousness that we are, as It can be focused specifically. Furthermore, there can be no doubt that the perfect order that is a universal fact is perceived and experienced in all our contemplation. This is true, whether our contemplation is, at the moment, the universal Consciousness contemplating Itself or the universal Consciousness focused as Its specific Self.

Now, we have digressed temporarily, but this glorious Truth must be presented just as It reveals Itself. Let us, however, return to our consideration of the boundless, inseparable All, which is ever active as our Substance in action.

When we consider the fact that the very atmosphere itself consists of what is called atoms, or energy, we certainly can perceive the indivisible nature of all Substance. It would never occur to us that the air could be divided into bits and parts of itself. Yet the air really is the very same Substance that comprises all Substance in Form, whether this Substance be revealed as the Form of the Body of Man, tree, bird, or whatever.

The Substance of what we call the Earth Planet, all that exists as this planet, is as inseparable as is the Substance that comprises the innumerable atomic structures which comprise the atmosphere. You will recall that all liquids, all gases, the air, all that is called solid consists of something the physicists call atoms, or energy. Here we have an example of the identicalness, the sameness, of the basic Essence and Its Activity, which is this inseparable Universe. So the Substance and Activity which exist as our Earth Planet is identically the same Substance and Activity which comprises our solar system, every solar system, every galaxy. Indeed, it is the same Substance and Activity that exists as this boundless Ocean of living Light which we call the Universe.

We have said that Life is everywhere because Life is *the* Everywhere. Just the other day, an article appeared in the news media which stated that some Russian scientists have discovered the moon to be a living, *breathing* organism. They state that, contrary to former opinions affirming that the Earth is a dead body, this Earth is really a living, breathing organism. This report was first published in *Tass* and now is appearing in our newspapers.

Well, we already know this to be true. Although they call it an organism, we know that the moon is living, intelligent, loving Consciousness in Form. And we know that this very same Essence in Form is alive and breathing everywhere. It breathes as the very living atmosphere. It breathes as the leaves of the tree, the rocks of the mountains, the sands of the desert. It lives and moves and breathes as the very Substance in Form that is this Body right here, now, eternally.

We have said that there is one breath of Life. This is the very Presence of the indivisible, conscious, living, loving Mind that constantly, infinitely, lives, moves, acts, and breathes. (My first revelation that all Substance breathes as one living, breathing Substance was experienced when I saw the rock walls of the Grand Canyon breathing.) The "breath of Life" is the Substance that is living Consciousness in action.

When a society that *appears* to be as materialistic as do the Communists begins to even dimly perceive the Omnipresence that is infinite, eternal Life, we find that it is wonderfully encouraging. And we cannot help but feel that our Consciousness of the indivisible Nature of all Existence—as we are in contemplation, whether during class sessions or privately—is at least helpful in this greater perception of the eternal, absolute Truth. God *is* All, All *is* God.

Here we have evidence, for all who read, of the fact that all Substance, all Substance in Form, and the *activity* of all Substance, or all Substance in action, is One inseparable Entirety. It is, indeed, completely one indivisible, infinite Totality. It does not exist as separate parts or particles of Itself. It exists and acts as one boundless, integral, unseparated Whole. This integral Entirety is the *sum total of all that exists*. This sum total of all Substance, all Form, all Activity is the aggregate of all Truth. It is the completeness, the totality, of every Truth, every Fact, every Existent.

When we have realized the inseparable Oneness—God, Love—of all that is the boundless Universe, we have also realized the indivisible Mind in action that is all Activity. This, of course, is this Universe—God—in action, and this universal Activity is as inseparable as is the universal Substance that acts.

Oh, Beloved, now we are perceiving the forever constant Fact that the Mind that is Love is our inseparable Oneness. We now perceive the absolute Truth that this Mind that is Love is omnipresent in and *as* this boundless Infinity that we call this Universe. Above all, It is present as the universal Body of the I AM that you are, the I AM that I am, the I AM that is the complete Identity of each and every one of us. This is a glorious Truth to contemplate. In fact, so-called miracles take place during such contemplation.

True it is that I have dwelt quite extensively on the ever living, inseparable, omniactive Substance that is this Universe. But it is only the realization of our necessity to clearly and completely *know* this universal Presence—if we are to know and thus experience this Presence—that necessitates this accentuation of the universal All that you *are*. You see, we are never going to be completely consciously aware of our eternal, immutable Perfection—in all aspects of our Being—unless we know just what is the Nature of the Universe and Its activity. This is true because our Substance and *all* of our Activity, right here and now, *is* the universal, omniactive Substance.

You are conscious right here and right now. There is nothing that is conscious but Consciousness. You are alive right here and right now. And as stated before, there is nothing living but Life. You are intelligent right here and now, and there is nothing intelligent but Mind. You are loving right here and right now, and there is nothing loving but Love.

Do you question whether or not the Universe is the Entirety of your Being and Body? Well, where are you conscious of being, or existing? Are you not aware of being right here? When are you primarily conscious of being? Are you not, *at this moment*, conscious of being, or existing? Knowing that Consciousness *is* this Universe, you are merely the universal Consciousness, or *your universal Consciousness*, focused right here and now, as your Life, Mind, Being, and Body. It is literally impossible to overestimate the importance of knowing, and often contemplating, the universal Allness that *You are.*

Oh, beloved One, do you *really* know that all there is of your Being and your Body right here this moment is the universal, conscious, living, loving Mind that you are, conscious of being alive and active as your daily experience and as your Body right here and now? Do you *really* know that your entire fulfillment of purpose at this focal point is really your universal, conscious, living, loving Mind, fulfilling Its purpose at this specific focal point?

Are you divided into bits and parts of your Self? Is the universal Consciousness that you are separated into particles of Itself? No! No! No! You can be assured that you can no more be separated from this universal All than you can be separated from your Self. You see, the universal All that you are *is* the *only* Substance, Form, and Activity that is all there is of you, right here and right now.

The only reason that we seem to have problems in our daily affairs is because it appears to us as though our *specific* affairs are distinctly separate from, or other than, our universal affairs or activity. The only reason that we appear to have bodily problems is that it seems to us that our body and its activity is distinctly separate from, and other than, our eternal, perfect, immutable, universal Body.

Once we know — really know — the genuine Nature of our universal Body, and also know that *this* Body here is merely our universal Body fulfilling Its purpose at this focal point, we experience *being* the perfect Body right here and right now. It is in this knowledge of being absolutely inseparable from, or other than, the Universe that we experience being the eternal Perfection that we are universally. And this experience is evidenced as our everyday experience and as the entirety of our bodily experience.

In our Bible we read:

> But, beloved, be not ignorant of this one thing, that one day is with the Lord as a thousand years, and a thousand years as one day (2 Pet. 3:8).

Yes, Eternity is *now*, even as the specific *now* is Eternity. By this same token, Infinity is *here*, even as *here* is Infinity. This very second, all of the eternal You *is*, or exists, right here, as every so-called atom of your Body, as every event of your daily experience, as the omnipresent, omniactive You that You – statement that Eternity is *now* and the statement that Infinity is *here*. That which is called time and that which is called space are identical. Eternity and Infinity are simultaneous, and they are inseparably One. This inseparable Oneness is here, now, and this Oneness, Beloved, is what you are.

Of course, the foregoing statements are only another way of saying:

Whatever you are eternally, you are right now. All that you are infinitely, you are right here. Here and now, all that you are eternally and infinitely, you are at this focal point of your eternal, infinite Existence.

Chapter V

Energy Is Indestructible

We have stated that the physicists speak of an atom as being minute particles of Energy. They also say that aside from these minute particles of Energy there exists absolutely nothing but empty space as the atom. Somewhere I have read that the atom is so infinitesimal that it has been proved to be impossible to isolate, or to separate, one single atom. This being true, if there were such a thing as empty space, just how much empty space would there be? Actually, there is no such thing as empty space because there is neither space nor time. So naturally, we conclude that all there is of the atom is that which they call Energy.

It is known that Energy cannot be destroyed. The physicists also know that Energy is equally present everywhere; thus, It is omnipresent. An interesting discovery by the physicists is that Energy always acts intelligently. Someone has said that It acts with knowledge. Furthermore, Energy is always constant in Its activity. There is nothing haphazard about Energy or Its activity. In the terminology of the physicists, this intelligent activity is called Laws of Energy, such as the law of gravity, the laws of chemistry, of electricity, etc.

Of course, we know that there can be no material laws, for there really is no matter. The point that really interests us is the fact that the physicists have discovered the intelligent Nature of the atom, thus, the intelligent Nature of all living Substance and Its Activity. Often we have mentioned the intelligent way in which the sun, stars, and planets function. It is interesting to note that the physicists have discovered this Intelligence in action to be the entire Substance of this Universe—namely, the atom. Of course, we know that the atom is the Light that is Life and the Life that is Light. Therefore, it is not so-called material energy; rather, it is omnipotent, living, loving, conscious Mind. And Its Activity is this eternal, imperishable, indestructible Mind acting intelligently.

Can the Energy that is God—Life—be destroyed? Can the Energy that is ever living, conscious Mind perish? Can this Energy be smashed? Can It be split; can It be divided? We know the answer to these questions. When even the most materialistic of the physicists conclude that Energy is eternal, it certainly should be natural for us to perceive the eternal Nature of all Substance in Form—and all Substance *is* in Form.

Beloved, if we are to transcend this horrendous illusion called the death of the body, we are going to have to clearly and completely perceive the eternal, immutable, imperishable, indestructible Nature of all Substance. And all Substance does consist of that which the physicists call atoms, or Energy.

Is Energy something that is dense, solid, dark, or heavy? Is It something that can deteriorate? Can It come and go? Can Its universal, constant Presence be absent? Can Its Presence be interrupted? Can It be any more or any less present? A positive "No" is the answer to every one of these questions. Thus, the very Substance—God—that is this Universe is immutable, eternal, perfect, omnipresent Light, or Life.

This omnipresent, ever living Light that is Life is the Substance of the Body called this Earth Planet. It is the Substance and Activity of every star and every planet. It is the entirety of this Body you call *your* Body. It is eternally present as the Body of everyone and everything, whether it be called the Body of Man, the Body of a Rose, the Body of a blade of Grass, or whatever. Yes, this ever living Light is forever present, constantly present, and equally, immutably present eternally.

Where does this leave a body that begins or that is born? Where does it leave a body that ends, perishes, is destroyed, or dies? *Nowhere at all.* And nowhere is this kind of a body to be found. There is no such body. It has no more substance, form, or activity than had the apparent body you may have dreamed about last night. There is no such substance to be in form. But there *is* Substance in Form. This Substance, however, is not the kind of substance we have seemed to falsely believe It to be. It is simply misconception, or rather, misperception.

Now, Beloved, if you were to ask, "Where is Life, Consciousness, Mind, Love?" your answer would have to be, "Wherever there is Life—and Life is everywhere—there am I, for I am the only Life that is alive. Wherever there is Consciousness—and Consciousness is everywhere—there am I, for I am the Consciousness of all that is conscious. Wherever there is Mind—and Mind is everywhere—there am I, for I am the Mind of all that knows, or that is intelligent. Wherever there is Love—and Love is everywhere—there am I, for I am the Love of all that loves.

"All that I know, everywhere, I know right here and now. All that I experience being, everywhere, I experience being right here and now. All that I am conscious of being, everywhere, I am conscious of being right here and now."

All that I am, everywhere,
I am right here and now.

Chapter VI

The Eternal Form

All Substance exists in and as Form. The fore-going statement presents an absolute fact. It is no mere theory. Rather, it is known to be true by the leading physicists. It is true that most of us cannot seem to see the Substance in form that comprises the atmosphere, but this does not alter the fact that the air itself consists of that which is called atoms, or atomic structures. A structure is form, whether or not it is visible to so-called human vision. (Incidentally, there are some of us who have seen, and do see, the indivisible structures in form that comprise the atmosphere, and it is no hallucination.)

The word *form* really means so much more than is generally believed. For instance, music has form. We have the sonata form, the fugue form, and many other forms in which music is written. One who has knowledge of composition can hear the form of a symphony, a concerto, or any other musical compo-sition. Furthermore, one who hears these forms of music could draw a diagram, or outline, of the forms he hears.

Now, why is it that everyone cannot hear and draw the forms in which music is written? The answer is that most of us have no knowledge of composition or of its forms. It requires this knowledge if one is to hear the various forms of music.

It is somewhat in this same way that it is possible for us to see the structural forms of which the air consists. However, there is a certain distinction to be made here. Knowledge of the form of music can be taught or acquired. At least, this is the way it appears to assumptive man. But the knowledge that is essential in order to see the atmospheric forms cannot be taught, nor can this knowledge be acquired. This kind of knowledge is always revelation, and it has to be Self-revelation.

It is true that generally this "knowing," or revelation, is experienced through study and contemplation of the Truth. But certain it is that never is this study or contemplation an intellectual process. Oh, our study may appear to be an intellectual activity. But let us not be deceived. If there were such a thing as an intellectual mind, it would not be caught with a book on metaphysics in its possession. Certainly it would not be interested in the Absolute. So, even though we may seem to acquire knowledge through the study of Truth, actually all that is ever truly revealed, thus known, is revealed in, through, and as the infinite Mind which is all Knowledge.

Often we have stated, "It takes the Mind that is God to be interested in the things of God." But it also takes the Mind that is God to *know* the things of God. These statements are Truth. Actually, there is no Mind other than the Infinite Mind which is God,

43

and this is true despite all the arrogant claims to intellectuality.

Now, it seems that we have digressed somewhat from the subject of this chapter, so let us return to our discussion of Form.

It is knowledge—through Self-revelation—of God, Truth, the I AM THAT I AM, that enables us to see the structures, or Forms, which comprise the atmosphere. But it is this same knowledge that enables us to actually see the Body of Light that appears to be invisible to most of us.

Of course, all Substance in Form is a Body of Light. Whether the Substance in Form be called a tree, a rose, or a grain of sand is of no consequence. This is true because all Substance *is* Light. Furthermore, the Form Itself is of the same Light as is the Substance Itself. If we seem to see darkness, density, or solidity, we simply are not seeing the Substance in Form that is right here. When we see—actually see—all Substance as Form, we are truly seeing the universal Light, which is all Substance.

It may clarify this statement somewhat to again realize that all Substance exists *as* Form. Perhaps we can more readily perceive the indivisibility of the Infinite Substance by the use of that little important word *as*. Above all, we must always perceive that there is nothing present as Form that acts as a divisional outline.

In our morning classes, as presented in Volume One of this set of classnotes, we have compared this universal, omniactive Substance, God, to a boundless Universe of living Light. We will not repeat here the revelations of our morning sessions. But it would be well right at this point to remind ourselves of the indivisible Nature of all Substance and just how, and why, It is inseparable, even though all Substance does exist in and as Form.

The Body of Light has been seen and experienced by many enlightened ones throughout the ages, and right today, there are many of us who see and experience being this Body of Light. Once this Body of Light is seen, and particularly when It is experienced, there can never be any doubt as to Its existence. *We know, and we know that we know.* However, it must be said that this Body of Light does exist as Form, but never does the Form separate the Body of Light from the universal Light that is all Substance and the Activity of all Substance.

Of course, you realize that the subject of Body has been of paramount importance throughout all of our writings. Perhaps it may seem that we have over-emphasized this particular aspect of our Being. This could very well be true if you feel that your Body is a good, healthy, sound Body right now — which, of course, It is — but there is more to this revelation of Body than we may realize at first glance.

No matter what your activity may be, in and as your daily affairs, this Body is involved. Actually, if there were no Body, there would be no activity. This is true because in order that activity act, there has to be a Substance that is active. Furthermore, this—and all—Substance exists in and as Form. Yes, this Body is essential to the daily activity of every one of us. It is definitely a focal point of our infinite Identity, our infinite, omniactive Substance.

There could be no complete fulfillment of purpose for anyone if there were no Body. Suppose you are a salesman, an engineer, scientist, etc. Could you fulfill your purpose completely if you were bodiless? Could an artist portray the Beauty he sees and feels if he were bodiless? Suppose you are a pianist, a violinist, or a singer. Could you practice, or perform on stage, if you were bodiless?

Jesus himself knew that the Body was necessary to his fulfillment of purpose. He presented to the people around him a Body that even they could see and understand. It is true that the way this Body appears is not the way It actually is. Nonetheless, the Body that is alive right here is the Body that consists of Life, and this Body is necessary to our complete fulfillment of purpose. The fact that, to those about us, It appears to be a material body does not concern us. *We know what comprises this Body*, and we go about our daily activities *knowing* what we are. However, we don't talk about it to those who apparently would not understand.

Jesus knew the Nature of his genuine and only Body. Actually, he presented this Body of Light to the three disciples, Peter, James, and John, who accompanied him to the Mount of Transfiguration. It was during that episode that the disciples also saw the eternal Bodies of Moses and Elias. This event is recorded in Matthew 17:1-4. It is the Body of Light that we are aware of right here and now. But to those about us, It does *appear* to be a temporary body of density and darkness. However, if there were no Body of Light, there could not even be an *appearance* of a material body. *It is the Body of Light that acts, moves, and fulfills Its purpose.* We are not deceived about this fact. Now we can perceive that the Body is necessary to our completeness.

The Body of Light is the eternal Body that consists of conscious, living, loving Mind. This Mind is Perfection Itself, and thus, It is ever acting perfectly. It is constantly in perfect government and control of Itself, and It never ceases to be in perfect order.

Now, when we say that this Body consists of Mind in perfect government and control of Itself, we do not mean that this Body is a little separate particle of Mind. Rather, we are speaking of the universal, omnipresent, constant Mind Itself. Really, it is the false sense of a separate mind and body that seems to bring about all of our troubles. But the perception of the indivisible Oneness of our universal Substance — *all Substance* — is that wonderful awareness that always manifests itself as freedom, joy, peace, perfection, boundless infinitude, and eternality.

Nothing ever begins. Nothing ever ends. All Substance exists in and as Form. All Substance is eternal Substance. The Form of all Substance is eternal Form. In short, the substance of all Form is eternal, and the Form of all Substance is eternal Form.

In order for anything to exist, it has to be known. Whatever is known to be, *is*. Whatever is not known to be, *is not*. This is true because all Substance consists of conscious Mind, knowing Itself to be what It is. If Substance in Form were not known to be, Substance in Form could not be. The eternal Mind that knows Itself to be all Substance in Form also knows Itself to be the Form of all Substance.

We are constantly more aware of the fact that the Substance of this Body is eternal. But we should also perceive that the Form of this Body is an eternal Form. The outline, delineation, which designates the Form remains everlastingly, and it remains forever the same outline. It is true that no Substance ever comes into being, nor does It go out of being. It is also true that no Form of any Substance comes into being, nor does this Form go out of being.

When misperception is transcended and true perception is realized, we know that the Substance in Form called the Body is eternal, immutable, and forever perfect. But we also know that the Form of this Body, right here, remains eternally and immutably the same Form. Yes, the very Form that is this Body, right here, is forever inviolable and intact.

An *appearance* of anything can appear and disappear. It can come and go. It may also seem to change. But Substance is not an appearance—It is genuine. Substance in Form is not an appearance. The Form of any Substance is not an appearance. It is true; It exists; It remains forever as that specific Form. The Form of any Substance can no more disappear than can the Substance of any Form go out of existence.

There is another very important aspect of the Substance in Form called this Body that we should clearly perceive. We know that the Substance of this eternal Body has to be perfect because It is perfect, living, conscious Mind, knowing Itself to be this Substance in Form. But we should also be sure of the fact that the Form of the Substance called this Body is absolutely, eternally perfect because the Form Itself consists of eternal, perfect Mind knowing Itself to be *this* specific Form. The perfect Form of all Substance is the only Form that can ever exist. Thus, there can never be a distortion of this perfect, beautiful Form. It can never be any more or any less. It can never be extended, nor can It be diminished. It can never be any more or any less beautiful and symmetrical. It is not subject to any illusion of age or infancy. It simply *is*, and forever It remains.

You will recall that Moses and Elias were seen on the Mount of Transfiguration and that the disciples *saw* the Bodies—Forms—of these two great Lights. No doubt there had been many friends and relatives of Moses and Elias who imagined that they had buried the Substance in Form of these two, long before they were seen by Peter, James, and John.

Well, we, too, can perceive the glorious fact that the Substance of all Form is eternal, indestructible, and immutable and that the Form of all Substance is also eternal, indestructible, and immutable.

Jesus, Moses, and Elias did not exchange a temporary body of solidity for a Body of Light during that experience. It was just that the eternal Bodies of Light that had always existed became apparent to the three disciples.

Sometimes, Beloved One, our eternal, perfect Body of Light is also apparent to those about us. It is seen whenever the Vision of those "seeing" It is the single eye—I seeing. If the Form of the Bodies of Jesus, Moses, and Elias were not eternal, the Form of their Bodies would not have been seen. If the Form of our Body of Light were not eternal, the Form of this Body would never be seen. Thus it is that we perceive the eternality of the Form of this glorious, eternal Body, as well as perceiving the Substance of this immutable Body.

Oh, Beloved One, if, at the moment, you do not appear to see this eternal Body of Light, please do not be perturbed or dismayed. You may experience many aspects of illumination, as stated in *You Are the Splendor*, and yet the Body of Light may not be apparent. Just be assured that your Body of Light does exist, even though It seems just now to be invisible. You could not possibly be alive unless the Body of Light were right here because the Body of Light is the very Life that you are in Form.

This eternal Body will be visibly seen. Actually, it is inevitable that It will be visible. Before the fallacy called birth seemed to overtake you, this Body of Light was the *only* Body you knew your Self to have, or to be. And even so-called birth did not change or extinguish this wonderful, perfect, immutable Body. It is here. It is here *now*. Don't try to see It. Be assured that It is here and that It may be seen when you least expect It to be visible. You are enlightened, or illumined, Consciousness right *now*.

If you were not enlightened, you would not be reading these words. So just calmly, confidently continue in the Way, and the Substance in Form that *is* will be seen.

Chapter VII

The Divine Economy

We hear much about the national economy, the world economy, the state or city economy. But never do we hear about the Infinite economy that comprises the boundless, immeasurable Universe.

It may seem almost sacrilegious to speak of this Universe — God — in this way. Yet when we view the Totality which is God from the standpoint of Infinite Mind Itself, we realize that Intelligence exists as an intelligent Universe. Therefore, there can never be an imbalance or an unbalance of the infinite variety in which God reveals and evidences Itself. Only that exists which is necessary to the Completeness, the boundless Infinitude, the Constancy, and the Eternality that is God. There is never a surplus in or *as* this Universe, nor can there be an insufficiency as Infinitude.

It would never occur to us that there could be a surplus or a deficiency of Life, Mind, Consciousness, or Love. Why, then, should it ever occur to us that there could be a deficiency or a surplus of anything that constitutes the Entirety which is this Universe? If we can perceive our universal, inseparable Nature, surely we can also perceive how impossible it is for a surplus or a lack of anything that is essential to our Being to even *seem* to be.

Of course, you know that you are boundless, infinite, and indivisible. You also realize that all that you infinitely are, you are specifically, right here and now. It is well to perceive the relevant fact that *only* that which you are infinitely can you be specifically. This means that what you are *not* infinitely, you are *not* specifically, right here and now. You exist as a boundless, infinite, eternally complete Economy, and this infinite, eternal Economy that you are exists right here and now as your specific Economy. You are just as complete right here, at this specific focal point of your Infinite Being, as you are infinitely or universally.

This infinite, divine Economy is present as every iota of your bodily Substance and Activity. This is why there can be no such thing as an excess or a deficiency of any Substance that is this Body. Neither can there be too much or too little Activity going on as this bodily Activity. There is definitely an economy of activity, or motion.

Previously we have often stated that *only* that which you are universally can you possibly be specifically. Right here, it would be well to consider the economy of motion, or activity, that is your universal Substance in action. You know that only that which is necessary to your eternal, perfect maintenance exists as your universal Substance. It is most enlightening to know also that only that activity, or motion, goes on as your universal Substance that is necessary to Its eternal, perfect maintenance. If there were too much activity as this universal All, there would be constant chaos forever as this Universe. If there were too little or faulty activity taking place universally, this Universe would have perished eons ago. Thus, there would be no Universe right now. This would mean that there could be no world, no you, no me, no existence of any kind.

Now, this very same perfect economy of motion, or activity, which is essential to the constant maintenance of your universal Substance, is certainly necessary to the eternal, constant maintenance of this Substance in Form called your Body. Almost any medical man will tell you that most of the seeming bodily difficulties stem from either too much or too little activity. Then, too, they may state that the activity of some aspect of this body is irregular or is not functioning at its *normal rate of speed or rhythm*. Thus, it is obvious that we should, in all our contemplation, consider the perfect economy of the rhythmic activity which is constantly and eternally present as *All* of our activity. Here the word *All* means the universal activity as well as the specific activity of this Body right here and now.

Thus far, we have spoken mainly of our bodily activity. But in order to live effortlessly and perfectly, the activity of our daily lives must also be perceived in this same way. The divine Economy of motion is present and active in and as every event of our daily experience. This is why we do not go dashing here and there, frantically trying to accomplish something that seems to be necessary.

For instance, suppose it seems necessary to purchase a new coat or some particular article for the home. Do we dash out and rush hither and yon, attempting to find the right article or coat or whatever? Indeed, we do nothing of the sort. We contemplate the universal Economy, knowing that this universal Economy is constantly present and active right here and right now as *our* activity. We certainly do not do any so-called "mental work" about this fact. Rather, we just consider the *fact itself* as it is.

Of course, we are always cognizant of the Truth that everything that is ever necessary is always present in and as our Consciousness. But we are actively aware of the eternal, perfect economy of motion—activity—which is our activity. We realize that there is never an excess, nor is there a deficiency of this activity.

Oh, our revelations may reveal many Truths as we contemplate such a tremendous aspect as is the divine Economy. In any event, when we do decide to make the above mentioned purchase, we simply proceed right to whatever article we have in Consciousness. We see it at once; we recognize that this is the right coat, article, etc., and there is no excess motion or activity. Certain it is that we experience no strain, uncertainty, or frustration. This, Beloved, is but a simple example of what it means to perceive the infinite Economy in and as our Bodies and as every event of our days and nights.

Knowing the Absolute Truth we have just been discussing, we do not go rushing about, trying to make the right contact for any business or professional purpose. We don't search dazedly for the right apartment, house, etc. We don't make a great effort to find the right opportunity, community, or the best employment. We simply know that we are the very Presence of the infinite Economy and that our activity is the manifestation of this perfect, divine Economy in action.

Chapter VIII

The Fallacy of Desire

One of the most insidious of all illusions is the fallacy called desire. To desire, to want, to yearn, or to wish for anything is to falsely deny that we are infinitely, eternally complete. If there were a mind that could be incomplete, this would mean that a mind that was not the very Principle—Completeness— Itself was present and was power.

The word *Completeness* is an exceedingly important word in our Absolute vocabulary. Of course, any word that states a universal, constant, omnipresent Principle is of great importance. It is true, however, that so many seeming difficulties can be traced to some false sense of incompleteness. Our point, at the moment, is to perceive the fact that because we are Completeness—the Principle—Itself, we are not really victimized by desires or incessant yearnings. Our Completeness is the Totality, the sum total, of our infinite Economy. And this Completeness, which we are, is also the Totality of our specific Economy.

Whenever we seem to desire or to crave anything, it is only that we apparently have not yet quite perceived our infinite, thus specific, Oneness, Whole ness, Completeness, as all there is of us. All desire is duality, twoness, separateness, and this always means incompleteness. Once we really, consciously *know* that, being All, we *are* everything that we could possibly seem to desire, we find that we are free from false desires. This, Beloved, is fulfillment, glorious and complete. Here we are not trying to get something, have something, or be something. We simply abide in and as the Consciousness that we are, at peace because we are the very Mind that is complete Peace—the Principle—Itself. In this way, we can perceive that we are that Completeness that is Peace.

We should be very alert about this insidious illusion called desire. We may have seemed to crave the more apparent so-called human things, such as excess food, drink, drugs, or tobacco, etc., and no doubt we have transcended these more obvious desires. But there are other aspects of so-called desire that are not so readily recognized.

For instance, we may wish, or desire, to be younger and more vigorous. Isn't this a denial of our ever-present Completeness right here and now? Isn't this an assumption that right now we are not the very Presence of complete, dynamic strength and vigor? Isn't such a fallacy as a desire for youth a denial of our eternal, changeless Substance and Activity? Of course it is—so away with such nonsense.

But suppose that some friend or acquaintance is so beautiful or handsome that we find ourselves desiring to be that same evidence of symmetry. Isn't this a denial of the Perfection that we eternally and constantly are? We can even be deceived by a false sense of envy by such seemingly devious desires. It is very easy to be entrapped by such fallacies.

For instance, perhaps John Jones is exceedingly successful in his business, and we feel that he just doesn't deserve this success. We might wonder how it could be that someone as seemingly materialistic, worldly, or worse, as John Jones could be so successful. When this kind of seeming envy appears, we are always inclined to make comparisons between our "goodness" and John Jones' "badness." Oh, Beloved, we are not going to be deceived by anything so insidious as envy or comparisons. We are not going to deny our own ever-present Completeness, whether this Completeness be eternal youth, vigor, beauty, success, or whatever.

Now, of course, the Mind that you genuinely are knows nothing of desire. It is only a false sense of a *born* mind—which doesn't even exist—that *appears* to be tormented by desire. So actually, you can realize and evidence the fact that the Completeness you are precludes the possibility of any desire to be, to have, or to do anything. No, it is never a matter of desire. Rather, even the falsity called desire is actually the Completeness that you are, signifying Its Presence.

Should some seeming incompleteness named desire appear on your horizon, you can joyously realize the fact that you are the very Presence of

Completeness Itself. You may find your Self saying something like the following statements of Truth:

> I am Totality Itself. I am the universal Infinity which is Eternality. I am Constancy, and I am ever consciously Completeness. This I am. This I am conscious of being. This I am conscious of evidencing here, now, constantly, infinitely, and eternally.

Suppose we should be asked for help by someone who seems to be the victim of alcoholism, drug addiction, etc. It may very well be that one of our own loved ones seems to be deluded by some addiction of this nature. Is it not clear that we perceive the very same Truths we have just been stating to be the very Mind, Life, Consciousness, Being, and Body of this one? Of course, we realize that actually there is no victim of these false desires. We perceive that the seeming craving only signifies that the Totality, the Completeness, that *is* this Identity is right here, now, and is revealing Itself. We know that the *only* Identity that can be right here is the conscious Completeness that knows Itself to be just what It is and nothing else.

This kind of "seeing" completely obliterates any illusion that evil really is something or someone, and it enables us to be compassionate and loving. It also impersonalizes the entire situation. It simply takes all false sense of misidentification out of the entire picture, and we see the seemingly deluded one as he genuinely *is*.

Does it seem to you almost impossible that this Truth would beautifully evidence Itself as someone who appeared to be so helplessly in the grip of some fallacious habit? Well, that which is called impossible already is present, and that which is present can and does evidence Itself. In fact, only that which is present can be evident. A complete absence of something can never be evident.

The previous statements will be most helpful as you contemplate them. Please be assured that this Truth has proved Itself to be true in innumerable cases or situations in which it appeared utterly impossible that the evidence of complete freedom could be seen and experienced.

Chapter IX

Here—Now

Often we speak of the Body of Light. Actually, the boundless Body of the Universe is Light. It is sheer Radiance—and Radiance radiates. We have a sense of the omniactive Radiance, radiating Light, and radiating this Light It *is*, equally everywhere. We know that this active Radiance is sheer joy, even ecstasy. It is *living* Love. It is Love, alive. Oh, yes, Love is a living Substance. It is Life Itself. Most ecstatic of all is the awareness of the glorious fact that *we are this radiant, living Light, being Its full and complete effulgence.*

Radiant, conscious Life is a universal Fact. It is a constant, omnipresent, eternal Fact. But to consciously experience being this Fact, or Truth, it is necessary to completely detach ourselves from all false sense of a past or a future. To perceive and to be the evidence of radiant Life means to be aware only of the *here* and the *now* of our Being. We must entirely disassociate ourselves from all so-called memories of a human past with its apparent failures, disappointments, and mistakes. Neither do we look beyond this moment to a "time" in which these so-called hurts, failures, and mistakes may be repeated. We do not even hope for a future in which we will be better, happier, or more perfect. We know there is no time.

We consciously live in the *here* and the *now*. We have no awareness of what we have supposedly done or been. Neither are we concerned about what we are going to do or to be. Our awareness is entirely focused upon what we are doing, thus being, right here and now. When our Consciousness is focused upon a supposed past or a hoped-for future, we are seemingly bringing a time element into the *here* and the *now*. Thus, the ever perfect, balanced, orderly *here* and *now* may not be perceived. It seems to escape us while we are looking backward or forward. When we are completely aware of *only* the here and now of Absolute Perfection, the evidence of this Perfection is perceived and experienced instantaneously.

In absolute Self-perception, we can say:

The whole, complete power of the universal, dynamic Energy, Light, Life, that I am is present right here and right now, and *I am this Radiance*. I am literally the full power of this universal, living current of dynamic, radiant, omnipotent Light. This Light—Life—is constantly surging, pulsating, and flowing in, through, and *as* the Substance that is this Body right here and now. This is why this Body is completely new this very moment.

There is not a so-called cell, atom, or item of this Body that is not surging, flowing, radiantly and dynamically, as the all-powerful, universal Energy, Light, Life, Radiance, that I am, right here and now. This is why fatigue is impossible and unknown. This is also why this eternal, living, radiant Substance can never deteriorate, nor can It ever be depleted. This is the *newness of the now*, and this is the *now of the newness that I am*. This is the ever Completeness that I am. And this Completeness that I am is eternally, constantly fulfilling Its purpose.

This Body right here and now is a perfect focal point where the entire universal, ever living, omnipotent Light that I am is constantly surging, circulating, and flowing in unobstructible activity. It is Vitality Itself, and I am That which is vital. I am completely revitalized, all new, this very moment, constantly and eternally. This focal point of my infinite Being is freshly activated and motivated this—and every—moment. Thus, this Body that I am is right now completely new. An entirely new Substance is dynamically surging, circulating, and flowing, right here and now, as this Body that I am.

Paradoxically, although this Substance that is my Body is the same universal Substance forever, yet It remains completely new everlastingly. The entire universal Substance—this infinite, glowing, radiating Light that I am—is continuously circulating in, through, and as this Body—Substance— that I am right here and now. This Body is Its ever new Light, Energy, Power, and Radiance, and I am this ever living Light.

Now, what is all this Truth we are perceiving? It is God—the I AM that You are—being All. It is All that You are, being God. It is eternal, constant, perfect, omnipresent, omniactive, omnipotent, living

Mind—the Mind You are—right here and right now. This, Beloved, *is* what you are. *It is All that You are.*

Ask your Self, "How can I, this very moment, be completely new and yet be aging or old? How can this Body right here and now be all new and still be getting old or decrepit? How can I constantly *be* the universal, omnipotent, ever surging, flowing, dynamic, living Light and yet experience a slowing down of the activity that I am? How can I be ever conscious *as* absolute Wholeness, Completeness, Perfection and yet experience any of these illusory appearances that are attributed to the body of man 'with breath in his nostrils'?"

I can't, and I don't know or experience deterioration, decay, or decrepitude. I am the Power of the Presence right here and now. I am the Presence of the Power right here and right now. What I am and know my Self to be, my Body is right here and now. I am conscious, living Mind that is ever surging and flowing as this Body that I am *right here and now.*

At this very focal point of the Infinitude of my Being, I am aware of being *All that I am.* At this focal point of the universality of my Being, I am aware of being absolute Perfection, Completeness, Immutability, sheer ecstasy, and radiant, living Light. At this focal point in the eternality of my Being, I am aware of being eternal, birthless, ageless, and deathless.

Here and now, I can know *only that which is here and now.* Thus, I can know, and experience, no accumulated past, nor can I know or experience a more perfect future. I only know that I am this moment, right here, all that I am infinitely and eternally. I can be no other, for right here and now, I am complete Infinitude; I am complete Eternality.

Timeless, spaceless am I. Birthless, deathless am I. Changeless, ever living, swirling, surging Light am I, right here and right now, This is what I know, and know my Self to be. This is all that I know, and know my Self to be. This is all that I am—to know or know my Self to be—right here and right now.

Chapter X

The Vision That Is

Although we have spoken and written much on the subject of Vision, we find that always there is more revealed on this all-important aspect of our Being. Let us perceive, and thus fully evidence, the Vision that is right here and now.

Often we have said that Vision is Consciousness perceiving and knowing what It perceives. We have no intention of repeating that which we have heretofore written and said pertaining to Vision. Nonetheless, it is necessary to realize that Vision *is* Consciousness. But now we should perceive that Vision is Consciousness *discriminating* in Its awareness of that which It perceives.

Of course, this discrimination of Consciousness does not mean a separation of the Substance that It perceives. But it does mean that Consciousness is aware of distinction of that which It perceives. Consciousness, aware of distinction, discriminates the specific aspects of that which It sees or perceives — in short, Consciousness discriminates in Its perception of the various Forms in which all Substance is evidenced. If this were not true, there would be no awareness of Form. Neither would we see colors or the various, although inseparable, activities of all Substance in Form.

Without discrimination, Vision would not be the fulfillment of any purpose. Now, of course, I am not speaking of so-called human limited vision that, in order to see anything, is dependent upon supposedly born eyes of matter. Actually, there is no merely human vision. But the Vision that does truly see, and discriminates in Its seeing, is this Vision that we experience and evidence right here and now.

Although the assumptive mind of man may miscall it human vision, dependent upon human eyes, we know that we *see*. But we do not see through—or because of—supposedly born human eyes. Actually, instead of seeing because we are supposed to have human born eyes, we see *despite* this illusion called the eyes of "man with breath in his nostrils."

The Consciousness that perceives and discriminates is the God I AM that you are. It is this I AM who sees, and It is this God I AM who discriminates in Its conscious perception. In other words, God is the only One who sees, God is the only One who discriminates, and God is the only Substance, Form, and Activity that God sees.

Therefore, we must ask our Self, "Whose Vision is this, anyway? Is this a separate vision that is possessed by one named John Jones or Mary Smith? Is this infinite, conscious Vision blocked off here? Is

It confined to a focal point called the body? Is It confined by these pinpoints called the eyes of man? Can the infinite, indivisible Vision that is God "seeing" be separated? Can It be limited by a delineation called this body or these eyes? For that matter, what is the Substance, Form, and Activity of these eyes? And to whom do they belong? Do they belong to someone separate from, or other than, the infinite, All-conscious perception that is God seeing?"

What are you, if you are not the I AM GOD THAT I AM? What "you" is it that sees? Isn't the "you" that sees, the infinite I AM God-Vision seeing infinitely, perfectly, and eternally? Is the infinite God-Vision that you are, dependent upon illusory born eyes? Or is this Vision the infinite, omnipotent, Consciousness that you are, seeing the glorious forms, activities, colors, etc. that It sees?

Above all, is this perfect Vision that you are any more perfect infinitely than It is perfect specifically? Is this Vision any more or any less perfect at this focal point of your infinitude than It is as your infinite Vision?

No! No! No! Never do we accept the deception that Vision belongs to born man or that It is separated into more or less perfect visions.

There is but one infinite, complete, perfect Vision, and this Vision is the conscious, living Mind that is the "seeing" Eye and that which is seen. Above all, you perceive that discrimination does not mean separation.

The Bible says that "the eyes of the Lord are upon you." Actually, the eyes of the Lord are the *only* eyes there are. The Substance of the all-immutable, eternal, perfect, conscious Vision does exist right here and now. This all-seeing Eye that is God seeing is focused, or is evident, at this focal point called eyes. It is God—the I AM that You are— distinctly seeing at this focal point. But it is not a separation or division of the infinite Vision that is God seeing. This perfect Vision always sees perfectly because It always sees Perfection *only*.

We realize that the infinite Vision is present— and *equally* present everywhere and eternally—*as all the Vision there is*. But we must also perceive that the Substance of the infinite, conscious perception— Vision—is the Substance and Activity of this focal point called eyes. If we can clearly perceive the all-powerful, ever perfect, omnipresent, indivisible Vision that is God seeing—not born man seeing—we should certainly evidence the perfect Vision which is the God I AM perceiving and discriminating. Yes, we should clearly perceive the incontrovertible fact that the Vision we supposedly have, actually, is the infinite Vision that we *are*, right here and now.

When we say, "It is God who sees," are we isolating you from this God who is seeing? No! Quite the contrary. What could you be if you were not what God is? What else is there for you to be? What Vision could you supposedly have or be other than God seeing? None. There is none other. So, Beloved, the Vision you have is the Vision you infinitely are, here and now.

Our seeming difficulty where Vision is concerned is based in the fact that we do not seem to realize clearly that *all Vision is infinite Vision* and that there is no vision that belongs to a separate person. But this same fallacy is our difficulty wherever and whenever any appearance of a problem seems to trouble us.

For instance, suppose something appears to be wrong with the body. Our question should be, "Whose body is this, anyway? Is it a little born, separate body that belongs to a temporary, limited person? Isn't God all Substance? This being true, must not all Substance be God?" Then we will probably be perceiving something like this which follows: there is Substance right here, and this Substance is in Form. Furthermore, this Substance is active. Because God—Perfection—is all Substance, then, this Substance right here is God's Substance. Thus, if this Body belongs *to* anyone, it has to belong to God. This Substance in Form is really the Body of God evidenced right here and now.

What am I? Am I not infinite, eternal, omni-active Perfection? Am I not the very Presence of the indivisible, immutable Substance which is God—the Universe? Of course I am; there is nothing else for me to be. Thus, this Substance that is right here is the very Presence of the infinite, eternal, inseparable *I* that I am, evidenced as Form, or Body.

Beloved, from the foregoing statements of Truth, you can expect to clearly perceive and to manifest the perfect Substance that you know your Self to be. But we must be vigilant where the perception of Omniaction is concerned. As previously stated, so much of our seeming bodily difficulty appears to be due to faulty activity. So we are always aware of the infinite, indivisible Omniaction which is God—the I AM THAT I AM—in action. The fact that the Body is inseparable from the infinite, universal Body makes it utterly impossible that this Body could have or experience an activity that is separate from the universal activity.

From what has just been revealed, we can determine the fact that neither this Body nor Its Activity is—or can be—separate from the infinite, all-omniactive Substance, which is God—the I AM THAT I AM. This Substance and Activity right here is merely a focal point of the universal Body that I am. A clear realization of this fact releases us completely from all of the undue concern about this Body.

God, the I AM THAT I AM, sustains and maintains Its own Substance and Activity in and as absolute Perfection constantly, infinitely, and eternally. It matters not what the Form of the infinite Substance may be. It is still the universal, constant, living, conscious, loving Mind—the God I AM THAT I AM—

being Itself *as* that Substance, that Form, and as that Activity. We have said so much about the Body that we will not tarry longer on this aspect of our Being right now. Nonetheless, it is well to perceive these Truths of the Body from many standpoints.

I am reminded at the moment of a wonderful professor with whom I studied music composition and harmony. He, too, approached the same subject from many and diverse standpoints. Sometimes he would say, "You must completely understand these subjects if you are ever to compose music." In further explanation, he would say:

> I'll first come in the door (of your attention), and if you don't truly see—perceive—me, I'll come in the window. Then if you still fail to see all of me, I'll come down the chimney, or if necessary, I'll come up through the floor or in through the walls. In this way, we will have all the approaches to this subject.

Needless to say, when we left his class, we really did understand harmony and composition.

Thus it is with us. When the Truths are clearly perceived that we have presented in so many various ways during this class, the evidence of these Truths will be completely manifested. It can be no other way. There are many aspects of every Truth. And certain it is that through the clear perception of one aspect or another, the Light will truly reveal Itself, and we will *know* and know that we know.

When this takes place, it is always that an awareness of some specific aspect of Truth has revealed Itself within and as our own Consciousness. It is almost as though some particular statement has triggered or released the seeming block. Then, of course, we realize that through the clear comprehension of one specific aspect, the sum total of all the Truths we have ever heard, read, or written suddenly culminate in complete awareness.

True it is that we do frequently return to the subject of Body in all of our study and presentation of Truth. This is necessary because the clear perception of Body seems to be more obscure than are many aspects of Truth. Furthermore, it appears that the Body is more personal—thus, more troublesome— than is any other aspect of our Being. No doubt, we shall again return to this subject of Body during these evening sessions, but let us now discuss that aspect of our infinite Being called Supply.

Chapter XI

Supply

Supply is manifested in many aspects of Itself, but just now, let us speak of Supply in terms of money. We have discussed this subject of money quite extensively in Volume Two of *Fulfillment of Purpose*, so we will not repeat what you have read before. However, subsequent revelations are wonderful, and they do present a viewpoint of Supply called money which we have not hitherto perceived. Therefore, let us share these greater revelations.

What is the Supply called money? We look at a piece of paper called a check or currency; we handle a few pieces of silver or copper, and we call this money. Now, as we have previously stated, there is nothing existing that is solid or dense. So the Substance of that which we call money is not what it appears to be. Nonetheless, there is Something here, and It is in Form. It is Substance in various Forms, and It has been named money.

Now we ask, "What is the nature of *all* Substance?" Consciousness is the *only* Substance in existence. Consciousness does exist in the Form of that which is called money. There is one Consciousness, as you know, and You are conscious that you exist *as* that Consciousness. Hence, the Supply called money is the Consciousness you are, evidencing Itself *as* that specific aspect of Itself.

Strictly speaking, you cannot possess money. You do not say that you possess the God-Consciousness that you are. You merely know that you *are* this God-Consciousness. In this same way, you can know that you are this same Consciousness manifested as the Substance in Form called money. The Consciousness that you are is unlimited. This Consciousness you are, being the Supply—in *any* aspect of Itself—is unlimited.

Beloved, do you fully realize that whenever we say the word *God*, we are really saying the God I AM that You are? When we say that God is the *only* Substance in Form of all Supply, we are really saying that the God-Consciousness that *you are* is the Substance in Form of all Supply. The fact that you are aware that there is such a thing as money means that you are conscious of money. Your Consciousness of the very existence of money is the very Substance that exists in the Form of checks, currency, silver, copper, or whatever.

Supply in the aspect of Itself called money is always present because It consists of your Consciousness, which is ever-present. Whenever there *appears* to be a need for money, it merely means that your attention is focused on that aspect of the Consciousness you are that has apparently become important to some fulfillment of purpose.

Never deny the Presence of anything that is necessary to your completeness, your joy, peace, or to your fulfillment of purpose. For this reason, it is well for you to perceive the absolute Truth that Supply, including that which is called money, is always present in and as the Consciousness that you are. So if some seeming need should appear, do not focus your attention on what *appears* to be a need. Rather, let your attention abide on the ever-present Supply, which consists of your own God-Consciousness.

You have accepted and perceived the fact that your Body consists of your very Consciousness that you exist. Now, it should not be too difficult for you to realize that any Supply that is necessary—in any Form—consists of your Consciousness that you exist. This is Truth, Beloved. You see, it is your Consciousness that enables you to be aware that you exist. It is this same Consciousness that is the Substance of your Body, and It exists constantly as the Supply that is essential to your Completeness. It is utterly impossible that you should be unconscious of anything that is essential to your Completeness. You would have to be only partially conscious in order to be aware of incompleteness—and you are completely conscious.

There is one more fact pertaining to Supply that it would be well to discuss and consider. You can no more be separate from Supply than you can be separate from your Consciousness that you exist. So often, you have realized that your Consciousness of existing is your Substance. Now be just as certain that your Consciousness that you exist is also the Substance in Form of anything that is necessary to your Completeness. And, of course, what is called money is necessary to your Completeness and to your complete fulfillment of purpose.

Now you can see how impossible it is for you to ever be separate from, or other than, Supply. And this Supply may be fully evidenced at any moment when your attention is focused not on the seeming need but on and *as* the very Essence that is the Supply Itself.

What we have been saying here is that your Consciousness *of* anything *is that thing*. To be conscious of the Supply called money is to be the very Substance in Form that *is* money. Be not concerned about money as such. Let your only interest be in the Principle—Supply—that is always present and limitless, even as your Consciousness is unlimited. To dwell on the appearance of money would be to mistake the *appearance* for the genuine Substance in Form that *is* here. The appearance can seem to come and go. It can appear to be present or to be absent. But the genuine Substance—Consciousness—which is your Supply, is constant, ever-present, and beyond limitation of any kind. Consciousness is all Substance. All Substance is Consciousness. And this, Beloved, is your Supply right here, right now, constantly and forever.

Supply is never limited. We are the ones who *appear* to place limits or boundaries around all Substance, and this limitation is due to our false sense of separation—or duality. One very subtle aspect of this limitation is the illusion that Supply is confined to just money. However, even that which is called money is not limited. We would probably be amazed if we were to know just what is the sum total of all that is called money on this Earth Planet. Nonetheless, there are many Forms of Substance and Activity that fulfill exactly the same purpose as does money.

For instance, sometimes goods or services are exchanged, and this exchange fulfills the same purpose as does money. Sometimes cattle, sheep, etc., are used as a medium of exchange. It would be well to consider some of these facts pertaining to Supply. To do this engenders a larger concept of the genuine meaning and nature of Supply.

All of us know that occasionally the welcome shade of a tree or a drink of clear, cold water from a spring is indeed Supply. Where is all this Supply? Right here as the Consciousness that you are and that I am. It is utterly impossible for you to be separate from Supply. Such incompleteness could only be possible if you could be separated from your own Consciousness. To repeat:

> Your very Consciousness that you exist is the ever-presence of Supply in and as every Form that is necessary at any moment.

Chapter XII

The I Am That I Am

I live, I move, I am aware of being in and as the Kingdom—Consciousness—of God. This Kingdom of God consists wholly of God—of the *I* that I am. I live, I move, I exist *as* the very Consciousness that is God, for there is none other for me to be. The Consciousness that I am is conscious only of being the perfect Substance that is God, acting perfectly. I am completely intelligent, for I exist as the complete Mind that is all Intelligence. This is the Mind that I am, conscious only of being perfect Substance — conscious of being all perfect Activity.

I, the conscious, perfect, living Mind, am the I that walks and talks. *I*, conscious perfect Mind, see, and I know that I *am* all that I see. *I*, conscious, living, perfect Mind, hear, and I know that I *am* all that I hear. *I*, conscious, perfect Mind, experience, and I know that I *am* all that I experience. I know that the only thing it is possible to experience is the *I* that I am, being. *I*, conscious, perfect, living Mind, *am*, and I know why I am and I know what I am.

I am complete in and *as* Him in whom I live and move and have the Entirety of the Being that I am. The I Am Mind is the Mind that I am. The Mind I am is ever complete. The Mind I am is ever complete

Perfection. The perfect, conscious, living Mind that I am is eternally, consciously, constantly aware of being *Completeness Itself*. Never am I aware of being absent from the perfect, inseparable, infinite, conscious Mind that I am. Never am I aware of being a vacuum or a distortion of the ever-present *I* that I am. Never am I aware of being other than the constant, perfect, complete *I* that I am.

I am the absolute Truth that is Consciousness. Consciousness is the absolute Truth that I am. I am the *conscious* sum total, the Entirety, of all Truth. I am conscious of being complete, for I am the complete, conscious Truth that *is* Completeness. I am conscious of being perfect, for I am the conscious Truth that *is* Perfection. I am conscious of being intelligent, for I am the conscious, absolute Truth that is Mind. I am conscious of being loving, for I am the conscious, absolute Truth that is Love. I am conscious of being eternal, for I am the conscious, absolute Truth that is Eternality. I am conscious of being eternally alive, for I am consciously aware of being that absolute Truth that is eternal Life. I am conscious of being immutable, for I am the conscious, absolute Truth that is Immutability. I am conscious of being beautiful, for I am the conscious, absolute Truth that is Beauty. I am conscious of being joyous, for I am the conscious, absolute Truth that is Joy. I am conscious of being peaceful, for I am the conscious, absolute Truth that is Peace. I am conscious of being infinite, for I am the absolute, conscious Truth that is Infinity. I am conscious of being inseparable, for I am the absolute, conscious Truth that is Indivisibility.

All of this I am, and all of this I am conscious of being, right here, now, forever.

Chapter XIII

Truth, A Universal Constant

A universal Constant is something that is always present, infinitely and eternally. A Constant does not fluctuate. A Constant never grows greater or lesser, more or less. A Constant is present everywhere, and a Constant is equally present everywhere. This means that It is present as equal intensity everywhere. This is just what Dr. Einstein meant when he said, "Light is a universal constant." Light *is* a universal Constant, and Light is Life.

Truth is a universal Constant. Truth is that, and *only* that, which really exists as a Fact. Every Fact is a universal Constant. The Truths, or Facts, that comprise the sum total of all Truth are infinite in variety, and they are certainly innumerable. But they are innumerably *one infinite Truth*. There is no way to number the aggregate, or Entirety, that is the sum total of all Truth, all that exists as Truth—and nothing exists that is not Truth.

We have stated that every infinite Truth is present constantly and present equally, everywhere. It follows that every Truth is a universal Truth. Yet every universal Truth is true specifically, so every Truth—everything that is true—is a specific Truth.

Sometimes, we may state this fact in different words. For instance, we may say that every infinite Truth is an infinitesimal Truth. Every infinitesimal Truth is also a universal Truth. This is why we can perceive that the atom is identically the same Truth that exists as the Universe, even as the Universe is the very same Truth that exists as the atom. Beloved, this being true, how can there be so much as one so-called atom or cell of your Body that is other than the Perfection that is a universal Constant Truth?

Eternal, living Perfection is an infinite and an infinitesimal Truth. You will recall that every universal Fact is a specific Fact. Thus, eternal, living Perfection is a specific Fact as every iota of your Body. Oh, if we can only perceive the depths and the boundless heights of the Truths now being revealed, we will perceive such great living Light! Really, it will be very helpful if you will study and contemplate much on this particular subject of this book.

Perfect Mind, or Intelligence, is an infinite Fact, but perfect Mind is also a specific Fact. Perfect, living Mind is a universal Constant; but perfect, living Mind—Mind alive—is also a specific Constant. Now we are ready to perceive how it is, and why it is, that God is equally present, constantly present, *everywhere*. Life is equally alive; Mind is equally intelligent; Love is equally loving; and Consciousness is equally conscious everywhere, constantly, and eternally. (Incidentally, the foregoing sentence is a tremendous statement of absolute Truth.)

We will also perceive why it is impossible for imperfection to exist, or to be, and why Perfection *is* and is All. Best of all, we will perceive the glorious fact that every universal Fact, or Truth, is the *I*—or Identity—that I am, that you are, and that *everyone is, forever*. For the fulfillment of this purpose, let us again refer to the atom.

We have discussed the atom previously, but it is well for us to remind ourselves just now of the facts pertaining to this basic Substance and Activity By this reminder, we can perceive further and more clearly the Truths that are now to be revealed.

The atom is supposed to consist of minute bits of Energy revolving in a perfect, orderly pattern around its center, which is called the nucleus. This center is also said to consist of Energy, and it is known to be Light. As stated before, Light is Life. Life is Energy.

The atom is Energy, and the Substance that is the atom and the Energy that is Life are identically the same Substance. Of course, you know that the atom is indeed an infinitesimal focal point of all Life. Now, the perfect Light-Life that constantly moves in such perfect order is merely the universal Life— light—focused as the specific Life—light—that is the atom. Needless to say, if the atom did not consist of *intelligent* Life, or Life that is also Mind, its activity would not be so perfect and so orderly.

We have stated before that all of the Substance which comprises this Universe is known to be atoms. And we know that all Substance in Form consists of the living, intelligent Energy which we call atoms. The Substance in Form called this Body is known to consist of atoms, and the Substance of the Earth Planet, in all Its completeness, is atoms.

This means that every planet consists of this same Substance and Activity. The air, the gases, the sticks and stones, the blades of grass, every grain of dust—all of this Substance in Form is identically the same basic Substance, and this Substance is atoms. Herein is revealed the fact that the infinite and the infinitesimal are one and the same Substance and Activity. They are the same identical Mind, Intelligence, the same Light—Life—the same Consciousness, and the same Love. But above all, let us perceive that all of this is the sum total of all Truth.

It is now apparent that eternal Light—Life—is a universal Truth, and it is true as every atom, every nucleus, every planet, galaxy, or whatever. Beloved, now you perceive *why* we are inseparably One. This is also why our Substance and our Activity are One and indivisible. Can you see now why our Substance is as indestructible as is the infinite Substance? Now you can perceive how it is, and why it is, that each and every one of us can joyously say:

> I AM THAT I AM. I *am* the Life; I *am* the Mind; I *am* the Consciousness. I *am* the sum total of all Truth. I *am* the All. The All is the *I* that I *am*.

Do you know that in order to exist at all, you have to be perfect? This is true because Perfection is a universal, constant Truth. It is utterly impossible for you to be imperfect because imperfection is not a universal Truth. *Only that which is a universal Truth exists as anyone or as anything.* If Imperfection were either a universal or a specific Truth, this Universe would have to be totally and constantly imperfect. If this were possible, we would have to assume that God Itself is an imperfect God.

You see, imperfection is not a universal Fact, so it cannot ever be an infinitesimal Fact. Conversely, the atom, which is the infinitesimal, being perfect, the Infinite is also perfect. If there were so much as even *one* imperfect atom, this would not be a perfect Universe—God. Yes, the Infinite consists of the infinitesimal, even as the infinitesimal consists of the Infinite. *Therefore, imperfection simply cannot be because it is neither a specific Fact, nor is it a universal Fact, or Truth.*

In other words, let us say that an abnormal growth is not a universal Fact; therefore, it cannot be a specific Fact. This is why there cannot be one iota of any substance or activity that is imperfect or temporary. Whatever is not true, not a fact, as this Universe is not true, not a fact, as even so much as one atom or one so-called cell. And whatever is not true as an infinitesimal atom or cell is simply not true as this Universe. If infection could be present or true as any substance at all, this would have to be an infected and diseased Universe.

Now, of course, such nonsense is impossible. But let us enlarge a little on our investigation of that which really does exist and that which simply does not exist and cannot be.

Any Truth, whether it be Perfection, Completeness, or whatever, has to be an essential of the sum total of all Truth. Only that which is inherent in and as the sum total of all Truth can be true, or a fact, anywhere or at any moment. This, of course, is true because all Truth, or the sum total of all Truth, is a universal, omnipresent, omniactive Constant. If the Truths revealed in the foregoing statements in this paragraph are clearly perceived, there should be no awareness, or manifestation, of anything that is not absolute Perfection here and now.

Let us now contemplate the way in which the sum total that is all Truth is perceived universally as well as specifically. In this way, we can realize that the *evidence* is inevitable of the Truth we know.

For instance, right now it appears that much apparent difficulty is presented by something that is supposed to threaten the Vision. This seeming threat is named cataracts. Is cataract a universal Fact, or Truth? Is such a thing a universal Constant? Is it omnipresent eternally? Does anything such as this abnormality signify Eternality? All Truth, all that is true, is eternal, without beginning or ending. Could such apparent imperfection be the Substance, or the

Activity, of the atom? Could such imperfection be the Substance of this—or any—planet? Is something called cataract a specific aspect of the sum total which is all Truth? Is it a universal Fact? If it is not a universal Fact, or Truth, can it be a fact at all? No! No! No!

If cataracts were true, there would be cataracts in and as every atom, every so-called cell, every star, planet, and galaxy that comprise this Universe. Remember, now, this Universe consists of the sum total of all Truth—all that is true, or a fact. If there were no Truth, there would be no Universe. If there could possibly be something called a cataract, this would have to be a "cataractic" Universe.

Of course, this would be ridiculous. Nonetheless, cataracts are inconceivable in and as the sum total of all Truth, which is God, called this Universe. There is not one infinitesimal iota of cataract or anything that seems to be a threat to our perfect Vision. Beloved, because constant, eternal, immutable Perfection is an infinite as well as a specific Truth, or Fact, there is absolutely *no* imperfection existing in and as this Universe.

We have realized that the sum total of all Truth is this boundless Universe. True it is that if there were not Truth there would be no Universe because this Universe consists entirely of every absolute Truth. The sum total of all Truth is Its completeness. Conversely, if there were no Universe there would be no Truth because this Universe consists of all that is true, or a fact. Yes, the sum total of all Truth is every nucleus of every atom, every atom of every cell, every cell of everything in Form, and the Activity of all Substance.

Now, you may ask, "How do I know; how can I tell whether anything is Truth or not?" Ask your Self, "Is it eternal, or does it have beginning and ending?" The answer is: *all that is true is Eternal.*

Then you may question further: "Is it mutable?" *All Truth is immutable.*

"Is it perfect, harmonious, beautiful, and symmetrical?" *All Truth is Beauty, Harmony, and forever harmonious.*

Oh, there are many questions that you may ask your Self that will reveal whether or not any Substance and Activity is Truth, or genuine Activity and true Substance.

Every seeming illusion of imperfection appears only as a falsity *about* that which is Substance, Form, and Activity. But it is well to realize that if there were no Substance, Form, and Activity, there could be no falsity told or believed *about* this active Substance in Form. Even a lie—if there could be one—could not be told or believed about nothing. Something has to exist before a lie, or an illusion, *about* it can possibly appear. There can be no lie about nothing. Something does exist right where this fallacious illusion about it seems to be, and this Something is the Body.

Oh, yes, Body is an aspect of the sum total of all Truth. Whenever we say "Substance in Form," we are speaking of Body. Even the Substance in Form called a poem, a musical composition, or a business is a Body. One aspect of this Substance in Form — Body — we are supposed to see; another aspect of this Substance in Form — Body — we are supposed to hear. But that which is called seeing and hearing are the same thing. It is all Consciousness aware of being what It is.

From the foregoing, you can perceive that Body is an ever-present aspect of all Truth. Truth *is* the Body. The Body *is* Truth. That which is true is the sum total of this — and every — body. This, and every Body, consists of the sum total of all Truth.

We have mentioned the importance of Omniaction in all of our contemplation. It is indeed necessary for us to clearly and completely perceive the omnipresence of all activity in order that our perception be complete. *Omniaction is a universal Truth.* If there were no activity, there would be no complete sum total, or aggregate, of all Truth. This is an active Universe. It is constantly active. Its Activity is always perfect. Thus, perfect, constant Activity is a universal Truth.

Sometimes it will appear that some particular aspect of the Body is not acting perfectly. Oh, they have all sorts of names for these supposed material organs of the Body, but actually there is only one name for the entire Body, and that is God. Nonetheless, it is said that something called the heart or the liver is not acting perfectly. Well, let's discuss this illusion for a moment and see just how fallacious it really is.

The Body is said to consist of atoms, and they have not yet found an imperfect atom. Neither have they announced that an atom was acting imperfectly. Of course, if there could be imperfect activity going on as the atom, it would have to mean that the atom itself was imperfect! But as you know, the atom is said to be the entire Substance of this Body. Now, since there is no such thing as an imperfect atom, or an atom that is acting imperfectly, how can there possibly be imperfect Substance here as this Body, and how could this Substance act imperfectly? It couldn't, and It doesn't exist or act as imperfection, So we realize that because every infinitesimal aspect of this Body is perfect and is always acting perfectly, this Body has to act in and as perfect Activity, through and through.

Nothing can obstruct the perfect Activity of this Substance in Form called the Body because there simply is nothing solid or obstructive to act as an obstruction. The perfect, ceaseless, rhythmic tempo of each atom, cell, so-called organ, or whatever is eternally established, and there is nothing in existence that can possibly interfere with, change, or stop this constant, ever surging, swirling, flowing, rhythmic Activity. The tempo of each and every item, or aspect, of all Substance remains forever the same, and there is no presence that exists or has power to resist this perfect Activity.

We have perceived the perfect Substance and Activity that comprise the atom. And we know that there is no difference between this Substance and Activity and the Substance and Activity that comprise this entire Universe. Now we clearly and completely know that it is this same indivisibility that exists not only as this Body but as everything called an organ and its activity; it exists as everything called a gland, a cell, and its activity.

In fact, everything called by any name whatsoever that comprises the Substance, Form, and Activity that is this Body, *is* the Substance, Form, and Activity that is the Universe. All that we have been perceive-ing this Body to be exists as an aspect of the sum total of all Truth. In short, this Body is all the Truth there is to be manifested.

Sometimes someone will ask, "How can you be so sure that all Substance and all Activity are so perfect?" The answer to this question lies in the fact that imperfection is not a universal Truth, and all that exists is, and has to be, included in and as the sum total of all Truth. That Truth which is true of, and as, all Substance is also true of, and as, the Activity of all Substance. Imperfect activity is utterly impossible, for imperfect activity is not included in, and as, the aggregate of all Truth.

Although we have been speaking primarily of the bodily activity, we realize that our daily lives are active and that our activity takes place in our every experience. For instance, there are many and various activities in which we are engaged when maintaining our homes. Certain it is that some of us are engaged in business or professional activities. We could not even make a telephone call without activity going on. So we must realize that this very same ever perfect Truth that is universal and specific activity is present *as* every action of our day by day affairs and experiences. Just as we can now see that there is no heart trouble, no gland trouble, no cell trouble, etc., so it is that we can realize that there is no business trouble, no professional trouble, no trouble in or as any activity in which we may be engaged.

There can be no doubt but that sometimes it does seem that an evil presence exists and that it is active in our experience. We do not honor this appearance of evil by asking why it seems to exist and to be so real. There is never a Truth perceived through asking questions about something that is not true and that does not even exist. Rather, our course is always to focus our attention upon that which does exist—something that actually is true.

A very fine approach to the instantaneous perception of the Truth that does exist is to question our Self in the following ways:

"Is so-called evil a universal Truth? Is this an evil Universe? Is there such a thing as an evil atom, cell, etc.? Is there such a thing as a universal Activity that is evil? Is there an active Substance existing as this Universe that is evil?"

The foregoing are just a few of the questions we may ask. And of course, the answers are so obvious that we need no confirmation of these answers.

There is no such thing as an evil substance or an evil activity. There is no such thing as an evil identity. Actually, as we now know, there is no evil at all. And even that which seems to be evil — and is not — simply signifies the Presence of the Good that is God. Yes, the significance of that which seems to be the greatest evil is the sum total of all Truth announcing and asserting Itself.

Now, it seems that many identities are supposed to be faced with so-called blindness. Well, blindness is not a universal Truth, or Fact. Is this a blind universe? If so, It would have to be an unconscious Consciousness because this Universe is Consciousness Itself, and all Vision is Consciousness perceiving what It is. There is no universal blindness; thus, there can be no individual blindness. Vision is a Universal Constant. Vision is included in and as the sum total of all Truth. Vision *is*. Blindness *is not*. If the Substance of the eye were incapable of seeing, the entire Substance that is this Universe would be incapable of seeing, thus unconscious, or blind.

The eyes signify the fact that Vision *is*. If there were no Vision, there would be no eyes. If Vision did not exist as an aspect of the Completeness that is all Truth, there would be no eyes. Since Vision Itself is perfect, that which signifies the Presence of Vision — the eyes — is also perfect.

Beloved, you can perceive this same Truth where anything of an apparently evil nature appears to confront you. Always immediately ascertain that unless anything that appears exists as an aspect of the sum total of all Truth, it simply does not exist. As you contemplate in the foregoing way, you will marvel at how quickly any seeming problem will dissolve.

Sometimes we hear the statement that one seems tired all the time and that he just doesn't seem to have any strength. Well, what is strength? Strength is Energy. Energy is a universal Truth, or Fact. Actually, the Substance and Activity of this Universe is Energy. You will recall the fact that all Substance consists of atoms and that all there is of an atom is Energy. This Universe is an omnipotent Substance, and this omnipotent Substance is Energy. The same Energy that comprises the Substance of this Universe also comprises the Substance that is your Body. Therefore, your Body consists of Energy. This is why you are so vital. This is why you are so dynamic. This is why you are so inexhaustible.

So, Beloved, if any appearance of weariness or weakness should ever tempt you to believe it, you can instantly be aware of the fact that this very Body Itself is comprised of boundless, inexhaustible Energy Itself. Thus, It can know no weakness, no exhaustion, and no depletion of any kind.

Beloved, we have used many words here such as *atom, cell, organ, Earth Planet, energy,* etc., and if we are not alert, it is possible that we may seemingly forget momentarily the one word that is important— *God.* Always we must return to this word *God.*

When we have uttered this one all-encompassing word, we have really said all there is to say. You see, words that we use in our attempt to describe or explain the All that is God are only verbal expressions employed for the convenience of so-called human beings, living in a world that is supposedly material. Naturally, these words have a material connotation. Yet we must use whatever tools we find at hand. But never do we actually describe or explain God with words.

God can only be perceived through an awareness that is *beyond* words. This awareness has been described as a "feeling." And perhaps this word *feeling* just about comes as close as possible to explaining our illumined perception. Nonetheless, it is well to realize that when we speak of atoms, cells, or whatever, we are really speaking of eternal, infinite Life, Mind, Consciousness, Love, and of course, all of this truly means God. By a frequent reminder of this fact, we are able to maintain our Consciousness completely free from any so-called intellectualism.

The omnipotent I AM Presence is the *only* Presence. The power of the Presence is the presence of the Power. The seemingly unseen Presence is all there is of the *I* that I am. The *I* that I am can only be

97

the power of the I AM Presence. I am the Power of the Presence. I am the Presence of the Power.

It is not that the Presence has *used* the *I* that I am to write or to speak the absolute Truth. Rather, it is that the omnipotent, omnipresent Presence has manifested—and is manifesting—Itself as Its own infinite, perfect, eternal, all-living, loving, conscious Mind. This is the Presence that writes these words. This is the Presence that reads these words.

Behold, the I AM Presence is All.
There is none else.

Chapter XIV

The Everlasting Body

It may appear that all that could possibly be said on the subject of Body has been said, but such is not the case. Actually, this subject, Body, is inexhaustible. We know that revelation is an ever greater and more glorious experience. And every revelation that is experienced is but a greater awareness of the boundless Body of the Universe. Thus, every revelation we experience means a more complete awareness of this Substance in Form we call our Body. Of course, we now know that this Body right here really *is* the universal Body, even as the universal Body is this Body.

Do you wonder why it is necessary to perceive more and more completely the Substance and Activity that exists as this Body? It is of the utmost importance for us to know—completely know—just what the Nature of this Body is because ultimately we must transcend this supposedly inevitable illusion called death. As we have stated before, *knowledge is Power*, and our knowledge of that which exists *as* this Body is the Power of the Presence of eternal Life. And I do not mean life in or as a temporary body.

Truly, the ultimate perception of Body is the incontrovertible fact that eternal Life does manifest Itself as Its own Substance in Form, and the Substance in Form has to be as eternal as is eternal Life Itself. We know that our Bible presents statements that can only be interpreted to mean that death—or its appearance—will be transcended.

For instance, we read:

> The last enemy that shall be destroyed is death (1 Cor. 15:25).

Then, too, we read that beautiful verse in Revelation 21:4, which says:

> And God shall wipe away all tears from their eyes; and there shall be no more death, neither sorrow, nor crying, neither shall there be any pain; for the former things are passed away.

Let us make no mistake about it; these are not idle promises or wishful thinking. Rather, they are statements of the absolute Truth that even *seeming* death is unnecessary.

Very slowly, or so it seems, the medical profession is arriving at this same conclusion. Several years ago, they stated that they could find no reason why this Body should deteriorate and die. And it is noteworthy that today some of the leading physicians and physicists are speaking hopefully of extending the assumed life of the body for a much longer period than has heretofore been believed possible.

Now, of course, we know that this is not the way to realize the eternal Body. But it does indicate the fact that even this assumed or mistaken sense of body cannot forever conceal the eternality of the ever living Body, which consists of eternal Life. Of course, we realize that all that has been said here pertaining to the opinions and hopes of the doctors and the physicists only serves to point up the fact that the revelation and the manifestation of the eternal Body is rapidly approaching. Indeed, this revelation and its manifestation is inevitable, and it is for us to at least begin to perceive and to manifest that which we perceive.

Anyone who has seemed to lose a loved one through that which is called death knows that there can be no Love manifested as this experience. This so-called "last enemy" is only the culmination of all the other illusory enemies that appear to precede it, such as birth, sickness, deterioration, etc. If there really were such a cruel thing as death, God certainly could not be Love—*and God is Love*. We have not only the right but the necessity to see through, thus to transcend, this cruel hoax which has been accepted throughout the ages.

Beloved, when we know—thoroughly know—exactly what is the Substance, Form, and Activity of this Body, that so-called "last enemy" will no longer be feared, nor will it even appear in or as our experience at all. Certain it is that we are on our way to the revelation of this complete knowledge of

Body. So let us continue our consideration of the Body that is eternally constant and everlastingly perfect.

Although this Universe is boundless, we can — and should — consider It to be a Body. Yes, it does help to clarify the subject of Body when we contemplate the universal Body. It is perfectly accurate to say that this Universe is the boundless Body of God. The Universe is eternal. It never began, nor can It end. Therefore, the universal Body of God is an eternal Body. From this you can perceive that an eternal Body is the *only* kind of Body in existence. This is true because an eternal Body is a universal Truth, or Fact.

It would be impossible for a Body to be manifested if no Body existed. And because the universal Truth — Body — is an *eternal* Truth — Body — only a Body that is eternal can be manifested. The *eternal* Body is the Body that is evidenced right here as *your* Body. It is the eternal Body that is evidenced as the Body of everyone and everything in existence.

We have so often stated that all Substance exists in and as Form. Well, when we realize that even the very air itself consists of myriad forms, in constant, exuberant activity, we can also perceive the eternal, indivisible Nature of all Substance. The physicists say that every one of these atomic structures that comprise the air is a Body, and every one of these atomic structures — Bodies — called the atmosphere is an eternal Body.

The universal Body is a constant, everlasting, perfect Body. Thus, perfect Body is a universal Truth, or Fact. It is included in and as the sum total of all Truth. Only the Body that is a universal Fact, or Truth, can be manifested.

As you know, every Truth that exists in and as the sum total of all Truth is an eternal Truth. This is why every Body is an eternal Body. By this same token, a temporary Body is not, and cannot be, a universal Truth. Thus, no temporary body can possibly be manifested. A kind of body that does not exist at all simply cannot be—and is not—manifested.

Only an eternal, perfect Body exists to be evidenced. This fact, Beloved, explains why there really is no death. This is why there cannot even be a *seeming* death. If a body could begin—be born—it would of necessity be temporal. This is true because anything that begins, if such were possible, would have to end. We simply *must* arrive at the point that is beyond birth and death. We can no longer gloss over the illusion that is called death by describing it as "passing on," "making the transition," etc. It makes no difference what words we may use to describe this horrendous illusion, these words cannot alter the fact that death continues to *appear* to be true and to be inevitable.

Let us not hedge about this illusion called death. Let us be as courageous as are our astronauts and launch into the seemingly unknown. Let us have as much faith in the eternal, birthless, deathless

Body as we have hitherto had in our eternal Soul. Of course we can have more than faith in this eternal Body. We can, through complete, illumined knowledge, be so convinced of the fact that this eternal Body is the only Body that nothing can shatter our complete conviction. *But we do have to really know what comprises this Body in order to experience such absolute conviction.* So let us continue our consideration of the eternal Body and why it is eternal.

The Body of God—the Universe—is beginningless, changeless, endless. It is never born. Never does It mature, age, deteriorate, or die. No born body exists. No changing body exists. No ageing, decrepit, or diseased body exists. Therefore, it is utterly impossible for such a non-existent illusion about the Body that *does* exist to actually be this Body right here. As stated before, the *only* Body that can be manifested is the Body that actually does exist, and this Body is eternal, constantly perfect, and gloriously fresh and vigorous.

Oh, this Body is a beautiful Body. How could it be otherwise, when It is the very manifestation of the Body of God—the Universe—and Beauty is God, even as God is Beauty? Beauty is an aspect of the sum total which is all Truth. Thus, Beauty is certainly included in and as the universal Body of God. This Body right here has to be beautiful because It is the universal Truth, Beauty, manifested.

Of course, you will continue to contemplate these Truths. Always remember that *only* that which exists as the Body of God exists as this — and every — Body, right here and now. Furthermore, this eternal, perfect, beautiful, indestructible, imperishable Body is the *only* Body that is evidenced right here, this instant, and eternally. This enlightened perception is wonderfully helpful to those of you who seem to be troubled with bodily problems. But it is also most helpful to those of you who are being called upon for help.

Now, in order that there be completeness in our perception of Body, let us clearly perceive that specific Truth which really reveals just how impossible it is for *you* to ever be separate from, or other than, this eternal, perfect, beautiful Body.

What is the Substance, Form, and Activity of this universal Body that is evidenced right here and now? *You are!* The boundless, irresistible, irrepressible, conscious, living, loving Mind that is the universal Body is what you *are*. This fact is why it is utterly impossible for you to be separate from, or other than, this manifested Body right here and now. Surely now, you can joyously say:

> I am everywhere, for I am the Everywhere. I am the Completeness that is this boundless Universe. I am the sum total that is all Truth — and nothing else.

> I am the Substance of all Form. I am the Form of all Substance. I am every Truth that is true, and I am only that which is Truth. I am the Eternality of all that is perfect — and all is perfect. I am the

Eternality of all that is eternal—and all is eternal. I am the Beauty of all that is beautiful—and all is Beauty.

I am the eternal Life of all that is eternally alive—and all Life is eternal. I am the Constancy of all that is constant—and all is constant. I am the Love of all that is loving—and all is Love. I am the Mind of all that is Intelligence—and all is Intelligence. I am the Consciousness of all that is conscious—and all is Consciousness. I am the Truth of all that is true—and all is Truth.

Oh, Beloved, all of this you can truthfully and joyously say. And you can ecstatically say much more that is true. Above all, you can now perceive that you truly are every Truth that you can ever possibly know. It is true that there are no boundaries around the Consciousness that you are. Only that which you are everywhere, universally, are you right now and here. Only that which you eternally are can you ever be. Only that which is your universal I AM Body is this Body right here and now.

You see, the Substance that is the manifestation *is* identically the same Substance that is the universal, perfect Principle, and this is the Substance that *you are*. In like manner, the Activity of the manifest Body *is* identically the same Activity as the perfect, universal Life Principle—which *you are*—in perfect, ceaseless motion.

The rhythmic surge and flow of the universal I AM Substance, Body, is eternal Life, or Activity Itself. It is forever irresistible, irrepressible, and unobstructible. *There is no solidity to obstruct It.* And this universal, perfect, ceaseless surge and flow is the I AM that *You are,* being eternally and constantly active. You are the rhythmic, surging flow that is *all* activity. You can never stand still. You can never come to a stop. This is why you have not and cannot accumulate any substance. You cannot possibly have remained static or immovable. Thus, you could never be victimized by the cumulative illusions of old age, middle age, or even "teen age."

Each moment, this Body that you are is entirely new because each moment the infinite Substance that you are surges and flows in, through, and as the ever new — yet ever the same — Substance that is this manifest Body. This is why no disease has, or can have, accumulated or can have developed as this manifest Body. The Substance of this manifest Body that you are can be compared to a constantly swirling, irresistible fluid, ever circling in and as this "eddy" of your universality called this Body.

Beloved, this is your evidence. This manifest Body *is* the evidence of the fact that You are an eternal, perfect, constant, beautiful Body of living, loving, intelligent Consciousness.

Chapter XV

The Evidence

And the earth was without form, and void, and darkness was upon the face of the deep. And the Spirit of God moved upon the face of the waters, and God said, let there be light: and there was light. And God saw the light that it was good: and God divided the light from the darkness.
— Gen. 1:2–4

If there were no form, the Earth would be void, for there would be no *evidence* of the fact that God, the universal *I* that You are and that I am, exists. It would be void of every evidence of Itself. This is true because Substance in and as Form is the evidence that Substance *is*. Form is the evidence that God *is*. Without Form, the Infinite would not only be devoid of any evidence of Itself but It would not be the fulfillment of any purpose whatsoever. In short — infinite, living, conscious, loving Mind would be purposeless. Thus, this universal Intelligence would have no purpose or reason for being. Remember, now: *You are this infinite Mind.*

The infinite Intelligence which *is*, does — of necessity — fulfill Its purpose in being. This is Mind, Intelligence, in action. If there were no purpose fulfilled, there would be no evidence of Mind, or Intelligence, and of course, there would be darkness — ignorance, absence of knowledge—universally. Absence of knowledge would mean the total absence of the Mind, Intelligence, that is *all* knowledge.

Total darkness, if such could be, could be termed mental blindness. Isn't this so-called mental blindness the way this world of little, seemingly assumptive men—struggling, fighting, arrogant, pompous, immature—appears to be right today? And to the extent that we are not aware of *being* the Light Itself, it appears that we, too, are comparatively blind.

Once we are aware of "things as they are," we are conscious *of* the Light, and we are conscious of *being* the Light. The Light is the Mind that is full, total, entire, complete knowledge. No Substance in Form could be perceived, or known, if the all-knowing Mind—that *you are*—knew it not.

In Genesis 1:3, we read, "Let there be light: and there was light." Yes, the Light already is—and always was—what It will ever be. It is our fulfillment of purpose to just *let It be*. We don t try to make It be; we let It be because It already *is* all there is of the Substance and the Activity that we are.

Yes, the Light was, even though the seeming darkness appeared to conceal or to obscure It. And the Light does move. It is always in motion, revealing Itself as the Substance, the Activity, and the Form that is all Existence.

> In him was life; and the life was the light of men. And the light shineth in darkness; and the darkness comprehended it not ... That was the

true light, which lighteth every man that cometh into the world (John 1:4, 5, 9).

If you will read and contemplate these verses and the verses just preceding and following them, you will realize that the Light is the Christ-Consciousness, or the Christ.

Man is God, being. God, being Man, is the Christ. The Christ is the true Light that exists as every Christ—Man—and this is true because even though he seems to come, or be born, into a world of darkness, the Light is the All of Existence.

Beloved, be very alert here; when we speak of the Christ, or Man, we are not minimizing or separating the universal Christ-Consciousness into many consciousnesses. We are still speaking of the universal Christ that *you are*.

But let us continue. We who are aware of being the Light *are* the Light that is the Christ-Consciousness, or God—the Light that is Life, *being* Man. Man is the evidence of the fact that the universal Christ-Consciousness *is*.

We, right here and now, are saying, "Let there be Light." Let the Light that is our Entirety reveal and evidence Itself as our Self. What is our Self? The *I* that I am is the only Self of any one of us. Of course, the seeming darkness does not comprehend the Christ-Light that we are. The darkness—ignorance —cannot comprehend anything at all, for it is non-mind, which means no mind whatever. But we—the

Christ-Consciousness, the Light—do understand. We do comprehend, for we are the Presence of the Mind that is all knowledge—whole, complete knowledge. And this is the Light that we are. Thus, we are the Light of the world.

Certain it is that this Light that we are is revealing Itself right here and now for the fulfillment of a tremendous, magnificent, vitally important purpose. We know that darkness, ignorance, hatred, and strife do seem to cover the face of the Earth. This is why we are contemplating these Truths this moment. This, Beloved, is why these glorious revelations are being evidenced right here. Yes, these revelations are being realized everywhere whenever there is open Consciousness. This is true because we know that our Consciousness is boundless and immeasurable. And the Light that we are *is power*.

You will recall that the physicists say there is enough power in one atom to sustain a man at hard labor for a thousand years. Well, there is enough power in the Light that we are perceiving, and being, to completely obliterate the *apparent* darkness that seethes throughout this world of appearance. The Bible says, "Let your light shine." It doesn't say to form peace organizations, to pray, or to do mental work. No! It just says to let the Light that you *are* shine. Let there be Light, and the Light that you are, *is*. Yes, the Light that you are was, It is, and It will forever be. Indeed, *you are this Light*. "Let there be light," and there was—and there is—this Light.

Beloved, you are this boundless, omnipotent, omni-active Light.

Right now, let us have an example of what it means to *be* rather than to *do*. To *be* is to be conscious that we exist *as what we are*. We are conscious that we exist as the Light. We know that the Light is Life Itself and that Life is Mind. We also know that living, conscious Mind is Love. Of course, we should be active as the Light that we are, but this activity should be an activity of *being* rather than one of doing. Frequently and regularly, we should contemplate the Light that is the Life of every man, even though he does *seem* to have been born into a world of darkness—ignorance. We contemplate the indivisibility, the inherent Life—Light—that is alive as every Man, although it does seem that mankind is steeped in hatred, selfishness, cruelty, and strife.

We are not concerned with what man *seems* to be. What is that to us? We are concerned only with that which Man genuinely *is*. In our contemplation, we perceive the boundless Nature of the Light we are and that everyone actually is. And we perceive the indivisible Nature of the Light that is Life. Above all, we consider the fact that this boundless Life that is alive as every Identity is alive as the Life that we are, and we also contemplate the fact that the Life that we are is identically the same Life that is alive as every Identity. We know that in and as this Light there is no darkness—ignorance—at all.

Oh, there is power in this contemplation. Sometimes we are inclined to wonder whether or not we are being any help in this world, which seems to be torn by hunger, cruelty, strife, etc. Please be assured, our kind of contemplation is the *only* genuine help that can obliterate this miasmic picture of the world. If prayers to God or mental work could have enlightened the world, this troublesome, tragic appearance of strife and suffering would have been dissolved long ago. If peace organizations or negotiations *between* so-called born men could have harmoniously settled the affairs of the world, then this world would have been peaceful, joyous, and perfectly harmonious, years ago. No! All effort that is called human is duality. And so long as separateness seems to be the lot of "man with breath in his nostrils," the long sought for peace will not be evidenced. It is our necessity to *know* what constitutes this world, and it is also imperative that we *be* every Truth we know.

It is obvious that when we contemplate these Truths, we are not doing something for the purpose of changing anything. To contemplate is to simply *consider*, or to view, the Universe as It *is*. We do not attempt to concentrate our entire attention and to hold it at any given point. The word *contemplation* has a connotation that is slightly different from the word *meditation*, although sometimes these words are used interchangeably. But generally, to meditate means to concentrate the so-called human mind at a given point or area of thought. This mental activity is strictly based on that which is called the human level. Oh yes, it is believed that it leads or expands *out* into a universal awareness. Yet it is, at least at first, accomplished through a mental *effort*.

In contemplation, there is no effort. We are not attempting to do anything. We are only considering that which is everlastingly done or established. And certain it is that there is no effort or work involved in our contemplation.

Beloved, this is why our daily lives are so effortless and so wonderfully harmonious. It is always the assumptive little "I" that imagines it has to do something or that it is doing something. The I Am that we are is fully aware of the fact that the so-called doing is merely effortless *being*.

Yes, all is Being and we *are* that Being. So in our contemplation, we are simply actively, consciously *being* the Light that we are and that *everyone actually is*. And this is true, even though few there are who seem to be aware of being this Light. But we know that we are this glorious, omnipotent Light, fulfilling Its purpose just by consciously knowing what It *is* and *being* that which It knows.

We realize the utter futility of any attempt to change, to improve, or to perfect that which is, by Its very nature, perfect. Yet, it does require vigilance to constantly perceive the perfect Nature of all Existence. Whenever we deviate, even to the slightest degree, from our conscious awareness of absolute Perfection, the illusions of imperfection can certainly appear, and they can appear to be very real indeed. If we seem to see, or to be aware of, anything that appears in need of improvement or in need of change, we are not really seeing, or perceiving, the eternal, immutable, perfect Substance and Activity that is always present.

Should such an illusion present itself, immediately we are aware of the fact that the *only* Mind we have, or are, sees and knows nothing in need of change or improvement. The Mind we genuinely are knows only Its perfect, immutable Substance, Form, and Activity. As we have said, it is always the assumptive— but nonexistent—little "I" that imagines it must do something *for* or *about* something. And right here is where the effort, the work, and the seeming struggle appears.

The *I* that I am—which is the *only I*— knows that all is everlastingly perfect and sublime. This *I* knows nothing of hatred and strife that must be healed, or exchanged, for Love and Peace. It is not that anything must change at all. Rather, the fact is that we perceive the absolute, ultimate, perfect Presence everywhere, eternally and constantly. And *this Presence is the Light that is the Mind that is all knowledge.*

Now, of course, frequently the question arises, "What about our boys over there fighting, being injured, and even dying? Can we just ignore such tragic cruelty?" No! We do not ignore the fact that these horrendous events do appear to be taking place. We know what seems to be going on in this world of appearance. We keep informed because it would be unloving and unintelligent for us to not be informed.

Even so, we do not have to see something that claims to be evil in order to know that such miasmic appearances do seem to exist; indeed, they can also appear to be very real. Right here is where we must be alert. We must be able to literally "look into the face of the devil, and see God." This quotation from (to me) an unknown author is one of the most spiritually perceptive statements I have ever heard. Our point is that we must recognize the so-called face of evil as it appears to be, but we persist in our awareness of the Presence of God and that God is the *only Presence*.

This, Beloved, is our way of being that which the world calls helpful. And let us not be deceived. Our clear perception of the Absolute Truth *is* Power. Indeed, it is omnipotent, living, intelligent Love Itself in action, and It does perform Its mighty works.

We do consider our boys and all of those who seem to be involved in this apparent upheaval. We are actively aware of the fact that they are completely immune to every seeming, unloving, destructive so-called force. All of us have heard of what the world calls miracles taking place right where the battles seem to be raging. It is no surprise, to those of us who are really actively conscious of these boys as they genuinely are, when we read or hear of something called a miracle.

Of course, we do not deceive ourselves by believing that we are the only ones whose clear perception is fraught with *Power*. But this is not our concern. What does concern us is that we remain constant in our dedicated "seeing." We know, through many evidences, or proofs, that:

> The Power that is infinite Love in action simply dissipates every iota of that which seems to be evil. It does this through revealing and evidencing the Presence of the good and ever-perfect God, who is the only Presence, the only Power.

Indeed, there is evidence of the fact that the perception that God is the *only* Presence, thus, the *only* Power, does prove itself to be true.

We know that the Substance in Form called the Body of every one of these so-called fighting men is eternal, perfect, living, loving Consciousness. We are conscious of the indestructible Nature of this Substance. We perceive the fact that "not one of them shall perish," for their Substance is imperishable. Neither can It be injured or in pain. Oh, yes, we are active in that which is called "the war effort." But our activity is entirely one of seeing and being the Absolute Truth that we perceive, or see.

When we perceive that which is true, clearly enough and persistently enough, there will be no more appearance of war. When little warring delusions called men realize that it is impossible to destroy the ever living Substance in Form that is the Body, they will see the futility of all warfare.

Right here is another reason why our knowledge of the eternal Body is so important. Actually, the so-called threat of nuclear warfare is but another aspect of the necessity for the full and complete revelation of the eternal, indestructible Nature of Body. We now know that the aspect of God called atom consists of eternal, perfect, living, loving, conscious Mind, or Intelligence. Certain it is that Intelligence would not destroy Itself. Any seeming illusion of Self-destruction is completely false because it assumes that Mind, Intelligence, acts unintelligently.

Infinite Mind must, of necessity, act intelligently. The omnipresent Mind that is all knowledge, by the very Nature of Its being, is incapable of acting unintelligently. What is the difference between the Mind that is this boundless Universe and the Mind that is every Star, Planet, Body, Cell, or Atom? There is no difference at all. Infinite Intelligence could no more act in a Self-destructive way as an atom than It can act in a Self-destructive way as the boundless Universe Itself. Intelligent, loving Activity is the *only* Activity, and there could be neither Intelligence nor Love in Self-destruction.

Only that which exists can be manifested. Non-intelligence does not exist; therefore, it is impossible that a kind of mind could exist that is devoid of Intelligence. Oh, we must go *all the way* in our perception of the fact that God is All, All is God. You will note that always we return to that all-important word, *God*.

Now, there is a point of great significance here that must be perceived since we are to realize the boundless, immeasurable nature of our clear seeing. The assumed brain of born man "with breath in his nostrils" is supposed to have a *spatial* circumference. Even the activity of this supposedly marvelous center of intelligence is apparently circumscribed by the circumference of something called the human head. But we know that Mind is not at all confined within the supposed boundaries of a born head in a born body.

Again and again, it has been proven that the genuine and *only* Mind is not confined, nor is It contained within the circumscribed limits of a so-called born body. Much less can It be barricaded inside the imaginary circumference of an assumptive born brain. If we really perceive the tremendous spiritual significance of these Truths, we can also perceive the reason why it is not only possible but inevitable that the Mind that we are is boundless. Thus, whatever Truth we are perceiving this moment is certainly not confined within the seeming limits of this Body, this country, or any spatial so-called limits of any kind.

It is well known by the astrophysicists that "time and space are simply so-called measurements for that which is immeasurable." Although they do not speak of the boundless, immeasurable Nature of all existence in the terms we use, such as Life, Mind, Consciousness, Love, they do realize that the Substance of this immeasurable Substance is, by Its very nature, indivisible. Furthermore, just recently, one of the leading physicists has said that the indivisibility of the Substance which is the Universe lies in the activity of the nucleus and the electrons which comprise the atom.

We have presented these views of the physicists for one purpose only: it is imperative for us to realize that the Truths we perceive in our contemplation are indivisible and immeasurable in terms of so-called time and space. In contemplation, we should realize the unconfined, boundless Nature of the Mind that we are. In our perception of the boundless, limitless Nature of the Consciousness that we are, we can be certain of the fact that our Mind, in contemplation, is present everywhere. Furthermore, we can realize that the Mind that we are in contemplation is fulfilling Its purpose *everywhere*, and because there is no time, this contemplative Mind is immediate in Its fulfillment of purpose.

Right at this point, it may be well to ask some questions of our I AM God-Identity. For instance, "Is it possible—God, Mind, being the only Mind—that such a thing as two minds could exist? And if such could be true, which of these two minds would be the Power? If there were two minds—which, of course, there are not—which mind would be limitless in its presence and power? If such were the case, would the greater power be the assumed mind that is supposedly born into—or even as—a brain that is limited by its own circumference and, at the best, to the circumference of an assumed human body? Or would the Mind that is completely free, boundless, and uncircumscribed in any way be the Power?

Of course, there can be only one answer to questions such as the foregoing. And because we know that which is true, we know that there is *one Mind only*, and this Mind is the *only* Presence; thus, It is the *only Power*.

Infinite, omnipresent Mind is infinitely intelligent. It is *the* boundless, immeasurable, omnipresent Intelligence that is so evident as the Substance and all the Activity that comprise this perfect, omni-active Universe. Certain it is that the *evidence* of this infinite Intelligence is present, and is *known* to be present, as this perfect Universe.

One might ask, "If this universal Intelligence is omnipresent, why is it that I do not manifest this Intelligence in and as my daily affairs and as my Body?

Actually, you *are* the manifestation of infinite Mind, in and as every event of your daily experience and as your Body. But this fact may not seem to be evident to you if you seem to be a separate substance and activity. All of the so-called problems of your

121

experience would be instantaneously dissipated if you were suddenly to realize that *you are this infinite, perfect, omniactive Mind, Intelligence, right here and now.*

Actually, you are the evidence of the fact that infinite Intelligence *is* and that this Mind that you are is the Isness of this universal Mind.

Chapter XVI

The Christ that You Are

Often, someone will ask, "How can I be aware that I am the Light that is the Christ-Consciousness?" It is a paradox that the perception of being the Christ-Consciousness is clear and complete when we are not *trying* to see, or to be, the Christ. The Christ is not experienced by thinking or by reasoning. We do not have to make an effort in order to be conscious. We do not struggle to know that we exist. We do not have to constantly insist that we are conscious. Rather, we just know that we *are*, and in this knowing, there is no effort involved. Beloved, our very awareness that we exist *is* the Christ-Consciousness. It is the Christ, aware of being and of being the Christ.

We are not ignorant. We *know* what we are. We don't have to limit ourselves. We do not have to accept or to believe any of the illusions of non-mind. True it is that sometimes our affairs or our Bodies do seem to be inharmonious. Such illusions can only appear for a little moment in the eternity of our Being, and because we know what we really are, we are not deceived. There are not two consciousnesses. There is but one Consciousness for us to be, and this is the Christ Itself.

This is why we do not permit our Self to believe that anyone or anything is imperfect. We know that we cannot be victimized by any illusory accumulation of inharmony. Even though the world of appearance seems to be an exact opposite from the Perfection we know it to be, we never, for one moment, depart from our perfect "seeing."

Jesus said:

> Verily, verily, I say unto thee, Except a man be born again, he cannot see the kingdom of God. Nicodemus saith unto him, How can a man be born when he is old? Can he enter the second time into his mother's womb, and be born? Jesus answered, Verily, verily, I say unto thee, Except a man be born of water and of the Spirit, he cannot enter into the kingdom of God (John 3:3, 5).

There is great spiritual significance in the foregoing quotation. What does it mean to "see the kingdom of God"? The kingdom of God is the Consciousness that *is* God. We know that to see is to be that which we see. It is the Christ-Consciousness that we are that is aware of *being* every Truth that we see, or perceive.

Jesus' answer to Nicodemus is very revealing. Of course, being the Christ, he knew that Man was birthless. But he also knew that Nicodemus was not yet prepared to perceive this fact. It is noteworthy that he immediately pointed out that he did not refer to so-called human birth. Certain it is that he did not mean that Man must be reincarnated or reborn humanly.

Water symbolizes purity. Spirit *is* Consciousness. The true significance of Jesus' statements is that we must perceive the fact that we *are* pure Consciousness. This, of course, means that we are to realize and to evidence our Absolute Perfection. The word *absolute* is defined as purity, perfection, etc. It takes the Christ-Consciousness to be so aware of Perfection that no seeming imperfection can be seen, known, heard, or experienced.

To be "born again" means to perceive that we were never born. It is our absolute, pure Consciousness aware of being pure Spirit, Consciousness, Life, Mind, and Love. It also signifies our awareness of being the eternal Christ.

These statements of Jesus symbolize many significant facts. One of these facts is that we are to realize, right here and now, the genuine, eternal, perfect Nature of this Body. We are to clearly perceive that the Substance in Form that is right here as this Body really is the Body of God. Yes, we are to know that this Body is the Presence of absolute, perfect Purity — symbolized by water — and that this Purity, embodied, consists of Consciousness, Spirit, Mind, Life, and Love. Furthermore, the illumined Christ-Consciousness reveals that this Body, right here and now, is the *evidence* of the eternal, perfect Body of God. And this eternal Body of God is the *eternal* Body that you have and that you are.

125

What does it mean to be born again? It means ever-present nearness, freshness, vitality, and boundless strength. Beloved, do you know that in this sense, you have been born again and again since you first began to read this paragraph? This is true because constantly the entire, boundless, universal ocean of living Light has surged—and is surging—flowed, and circulated in, through, and *as* this ever new Body.

It is noteworthy that the physicists are becoming more and more aware of the ever new Body. Not too many years ago, they believed that the Body was all new every seven years. Then they became convinced that the Body was renewed every two years. Now they have concluded that it—the Body—is all new every six months.

We know there is no time. There will come a day when the physicists will realize that this Body is constantly, consciously new. This Truth is what it means to be born again. Rebirth is a constant experience. You are the experience, and you are the experiencer. The Christ is not Bodyless. Illumined Christ-Consciousness reveals the Body of Light. The Body of Light is the Body of the Christ, or the Christ-Consciousness, in Form *as* this Body.

Jesus was fully aware of having, and being, the Body of the Christ, or the Christ-Body. His reference to being born again merely meant that all of us are to perceive that we have, and are, the Christ-Body. He knew—and knows—that the Substance that is this Body is identically the same basic Substance that comprises all that is called the atmosphere, all so-called liquids, gases, etc. In short, Jesus knew the completely indivisible Nature of all Substance. But be assured, he knew that this eternal, perfect Substance, existing in Form as the focal point called the Body of Man, really is the Presence of God being the Body of God, or the Christ-Body.

We could continue ad infinitum in our revelations of this subject, but these glorious Truths are already present in and as the Consciousness that you are. Just now, let us contemplate the glorious Oneness that is the Body of God being the Christ-Body and the Body of the Christ being the Body of God.

That which is the universal Body I am is the specific Body I am. That which is the specific Body I am is the universal Body I am. The foregoing statements may *appear* to be merely intellectual statements of facts, but indeed, no intellectual mind—if such there were—could perceive these Truths.

Beloved, pause for a moment and experience the fire, the supreme joy, the pure ecstasy of this glorious revelation.

Chapter XVII

The "I Am" Contemplation

That which is the Body of the Father I am is the Body of the Son I am. That which is the Body of the Son I am is the Body of the Father I am. The Father and I are *One* and the same *One*. I and the Father are *One* and the same *One*.

The Substance of the Father I am is the Substance of the Son I am. The Substance of the Son I am is the Substance of the Father I am. The Activity of the Father I am is the Activity of the Son I am. The Activity of the Son I am is the Activity of the Father I am. The Body of the Father I am is the Body of the Son I am. The Body of the Son I am is the Body of the Father I am.

Thou seest the Father, thou seest me. Thou seest me, thou seest the Father. Thou seest me, thou seest the Father being the Son. Thou seest the Father being the Son, thou seest the Son being the Father. This is the Christ I AM. This is the I AM Christ.

I am vibrant, dynamic, exuberant Life. I am living Love. I am Mind that is alive. I am Consciousness that is Life everlasting. I am all the boundless immensities. I am the Presence of all that is this boundless Infinitude. The Father and the Son are the same *One*, and I am that *One*.

Truly, when Jesus said, "I and my Father are one" (John 10:30), he was really saying that the Infinite *I* that I am, Father, is this focal point of the Infinite I AM, Son. The immeasurable, omnipresent, omnipotent *I* that I am, Father, is the limitless, omnipresent, omnipotent *I* that I am, Son. The infinite, constant Wholeness, Completeness, Allness that I am, Father, is the infinite, constant, eternal Wholeness, Allness, Completeness that I, the Son, am. *I*, the Father, am *I*, the Son. *I*, the Son, am *I*, the Father.

I, the Father, am the Substance and Activity of *I*, the Son. *I*, the Son, am the Substance and Activity of *I*, the Father.

I, the Father, am total, whole, complete as *I*, the Son. *I*, the Son, am total, whole, complete as *I*, the Father. *I*, the Father, am total, complete, constant, eternal Perfection as *I*, the Father.

I, the Father, can know only that which *I*, the Son, knows. *I*, the Son, can know only that which *I*, the Father, knows. *I*, the Father, am complete Mind, all knowledge, as *I*, the Son. *I*, the Son, am complete Mind, all knowledge, as *I*, the Father.

I, the Father, am omnipotent, omnipresent, eternal Life as *I*, the Son. *I*, the Son, am omnipotent, omnipresent, eternal Life as *I*, the Father.

I, the Father, am omnipotent, irresistible Love as *I*, the Son. *I*, the Son, am omnipotent, omnipresent, irresistible Love as *I*, the Father.

I, the Father, am conscious of being the *I* that *I* am as the Son. *I*, the Son, am conscious of being the *I* that *I* am as *I*, the Father.

Beloved, all of this contemplation is but one way of saying, God — the All — is the Christ. The Christ is the All that God is. The Body of God is the Christ-Body, or the Body of the Christ. The Body of the Christ is the Body of God, or the God-Body. This means that *all* that God is, is present right here and now as *all* that You are. It also means that *all* that You are is infinitely, eternally, and constantly present as *all* that God is.

Herein is your Totality. Herein is your Completeness. Herein is your God I AM. Herein is your I AM God.

Chapter XVIII

The Unobstructed Universal *I*

Beloved, the boundless Infinity that *You are* is, of course, this unobstructed Universe. It is the boundless Immensity which we have called the Body of God. The constant, eternal, universal Body that You are is ever circling, flowing, swirling, and surging as your unobstructed, *free* Activity. All of your Activity, all of your Substance in action, is, as you know, the conscious, living, loving Mind that You are in action. You know that the universal Consciousness that You are is the Form of all Substance. You also know that this same universal Consciousness that You are is the *living, intelligent, ever active Substance of all Form.*

Of course, you realize that it is necessary to briefly recapitulate here. This recapitulation is essential in order to clearly perceive the revelations that are to follow. Right here, it would be well for you to remind your Self of a few *essential basic facts.*

The Substance in Form, and in action, called stars, planets, grains of sand, blades of grass, cells, atoms, etc., truly cannot be solid, dark, or dense. There is not one iota of solidity in and as this Universe. It is utterly impossible that the universal Consciousness—Light—that You are should form Itself into something dense or dark that can obstruct either your universal or your specific Activity. Consciousness, being Light, Life, Mind, Love, cannot exist in form as something that is dark, dense, or solid.

Now, it is true that if there were solidity, your universal, thus your specific, Activity could be hindered or obstructed. But if you contemplate the Bodies of the stars and planets, you will clearly realize that there is nothing existing as these so-called heavenly bodies that interferes with — or obstructs in any way — the ceaseless motion that is this universal I AM that You are, in action.

Despite this fact, it sometimes *appears* that this universal Activity that You are can be obstructed in and as this specific Body right here. It is this particular illusion that makes it imperative for us to discuss some seemingly bodily difficulties. But even worse than this necessity is the necessity for using some words that the medical profession has coined for their purposes. So please understand that in using these medical phrases we are not referring to the Body that *is*, even though we must use some of these so-called physical terms. So let us get on with that which is required.

No doubt it would surprise most of us if we realized how numerous are the bodily diseases that the doctors say are attributable to faulty activity. Here are the medical names for just a few of these so-called bodily ailments. They say that high blood pressure, all so-called heart trouble, certain types of arthritis, varicose veins, clots, any impaction of any kind, infections—oh, let us not continue with these meaningless terms. Suffice it to realize that in one way or another, every *seeming* ailment of the apparent body involves the illusion that activity is faulty.

There are several ways in which our bodily activity is said to be impaired. It can appear to be accelerated, retarded, or uncontrolled. This bodily activity is even said to go berserk, or it may be claimed that it has come to a complete stop. However, the term most commonly used for imperfect activity is that it is obstructed. It is this word *obstructed* or some derivative of it that we will now consider. During this consideration, we are to realize just how it is, and why it is, that any obstructed activity is utterly impossible.

We know that the body is supposed to have a circulatory system. This circulatory system is said to be channeled throughout the entire body. Even the very skin itself is included in this channeled circulation. Let us not be too technical here, lest it appear that we are speaking of a substance or activity that really does exist. All that is necessary is that we perceive the general terminology used in this connection and the nature of that which it is supposed to describe.

The word *channel* infers a more or less restricted —yet extended—enclosure through which some substance is supposed to flow. The substance that flows through the channel is imagined to be confined *within* the restrictive walls or enclosure of the channel. But this is not all. The substance that constitutes the walls is supposed to be something different from that which is said to be confined within the walls of the aforesaid channel.

Furthermore, the so-called walls of the channel are supposed to exclude the presence of whatever is believed to be outside the channel. It is in these supposed enclosed channels that the circulatory activity is said to sometimes become retarded, accelerated, or obstructed. Furthermore, these channels are believed to be capable of hardening or even of closing.

If there were forms or delineations called channels, through which Consciousness flows, *what would be the difference between the flowing substance and the channel through which this substance flowed?*

Consciousness is the *only* Substance, and there is *only one* indivisible Consciousness. Therefore, the so-called channel and that which flows through it are identically the same Substance — Consciousness. There simply is no divided Consciousness, and this is true no matter what terms are used in order to symbolize Its Substance, Form, and Activity.

Inseparable Consciousness in Form may be called a star, a planet, a blade of grass with its many veins, a grain of sand, an artery, or an atom. But not one of these descriptive terms alters the fact that all Substance in Form is identically the same Consciousness.

Furthermore, the Activity of all Substance in Form is identically the same *inseparable* Activity.

Consciousness *flowing* is the Substance of the supposed enclosure, or channel. But Consciousness, irresistibly surging and flowing, is also the Substance of that which is said to flow *through* the channel. It is well to perceive that the Substance of that which is called the channel is also the very same irrepressible, unobstructible, ever active, ever moving Substance as is the Substance of that which flows in unobstructed activity through the channel.

Of course, you may wonder just what is the distinction between that which is called the channel — vein, cell, atom, or whatever — and the Substance that is said to flow through this supposed enclosure. Well, there is distinction, although there is no difference in the Substance. The distinction lies in the Activity of all Consciousness.

In order to clarify the foregoing statements, let us again refer to our simile of the boundless ocean of living Light and the innumerable eddies which comprise Its entire Substance and Activity.

During our exploration of this simile, we realized that the form, or outline, of an eddy did not at all separate the ever circling Essence of the ocean. And we perceived that this infinite ocean remained indivisibly *One*, whether it was focused as the Substance of the eddy or whether it was focused as the Substance of the Form, or outline, of the eddy.

We also perceived that the *distinction* of the eddy as its Form, or outline, was due entirely to the fact that the water circled, surged, and flowed at a *distinct* rhythmic tempo. But above all, we became aware of the glorious Truth that innumerable rhythmic tempos of activity were absolutely inseparable, and this inseparability remained intact, whether these rhythmic activities were focused and active as the Substance of the ocean or whether they were focused as a star, planet, this Body, a cell, or an atom. It was in this way that we perceived the inseparability of all Substance, as well as the indivisible Activity of an outline or as the Substance that circles and flows throughout the outline or Form.

These very same Truths are true, or facts, of every form or channel of this Body. The specific, rhythmic tempo of every atom, cell, star, or planet remains eternally the very same rhythmic tempo. It never accelerates. It cannot be retarded. It can never be challenged or hindered, nor can it ever come to a stop.

> Particularly right now, we are to realize that each specific, rhythmic tempo continues as that tempo throughout all of Infinity and Eternity.

This Truth, Beloved, is why it is utterly impossible for the tempo of any of this bodily Substance to be obstructed.

You see, the Substance of the channel, or form, through which something is supposed to flow or circulate is due to the distinct, *eternal*, rhythmic tempo which is everlastingly established as that specific Substance which *is* that specific Form. Indeed, the forever indivisible, universal Substance constantly and eternally surges, circles, and flows at every specific rhythmic tempo in, through, and as every outline, form, channel, or whatever. But this very same universal, rhythmic myriad of specific, rhythmic tempos forever and constantly surges and flows for the fulfillment of every purpose that is necessary to the sum total of all purpose. The sum total of all purpose is the eternal, boundless, omniactive Infinity, fulfilling Its boundless, eternal, constant purpose in being.

True it is that in the world of appearance there seems to be much belief in—and fear of—many bodily illusions. Some of the various fears have to do with that which the doctors call heart trouble, high blood pressure, and even something they call arteries, which can harden, thus obstruct the perfect, rhythmic tempo of the ever surging Substance of this entire Body.

Beloved, when the foregoing revelations are completely clear as your own Consciousness, you will surely know the complete fallacy of *any* supposed faulty activity. You will clearly perceive that no such things as those called obstructions, clots, or whatever can possibly be. You will really *know* that no activity in or as this Body can ever be faster or slower. Thus, there can never be *any* obstruction to one iota of your Activity.

As we have stated previously, it is in this second volume of our classwork that we are to perceive the *evidence* of the universal Truths that we have realized during the first volume of this work. Much of the evidence has to do with the Body. This fact is why we refer again and again to the Body. Every consultant or practitioner knows that most of the seeming problems which are presented to him have to do with the Body. For those of you who are said to be "helping others," I feel that it is wisdom to speak in terms that sound entirely materialistic. But you will know that *this Body right here is eternal, birthless, changeless, ageless, deathless and that the Perfection that is this Body eternally and constantly remains intact.* Nonetheless, I must now speak in the terminology that seems necessary at the moment.

You realize that, in speaking of the bodily activity, I have referred mainly to that which the world of appearance calls the flow of the blood through the so-called veins and arteries. But there are other areas of this body in which the activity can seem to be obstructed.

For instance, the activity called breathing can appear to be obstructed; the activity called digestion or elimination can also be said to be obstructed. The so-called veins and arteries are but two of many, even innumerable, channels in and as which bodily activity functions.

You could consider the aspects of body called the stomach, the lungs, the head, the heart as channels through which this bodily substance flows. And, of course, any eliminative aspect of the body would also be considered a channel. Now that we have used this obnoxious terminology, we can again speak more authentically of the Body that *is*.

No matter what aspect or channel of the Body may seem to be obstructed, you will now perceive that any obstructed activity is utterly impossible. There are various aspects of Truth, as stated in this chapter, which reveal how it is, and why it is, that every channel of the Body is completely unobstruc-tible. For instance, because this entire Body consists of Consciousness, there is nothing solid that can obstruct Its action or activity.

Then, too, there are the following all-important facts. The Substance of the so-called channels through which the Substance of the Body flows is also the Substance that is the entire Body. These channels consist of the very same Essence as that which is said to flow *through* these channels. Therefore, these so-called channels are not enclosures which confine the flowing Essence within the channel. The only distinction between the channel and that which is surging and flowing around, through, and as the ever moving Essence Itself is that of the various rhythmic tempos. And, of course, there is nothing about these rhythmic tempos which can possibly constitute a solid, confining enclosure.

Then, too, of the utmost importance is the fact that the Consciousness which comprises this entire Body is indivisible. Therefore, there are no divided parts of this Body. Neither are there separate or separated functions or activities. But this word *indivisible* has a far greater connotation than just the inseparability of the Essence in Form which is this Body.

This Body is absolutely inseparable from the entire, boundless, universal Body. There is never any activity going on in, through, or as this Body that is not going on in, through, and as the universal Body that *You are*. So you can see that we have again arrived at the Fact of your boundless, universal, omniactive Being.

It is in this revelation, beloved One, that you perceive how it is, and why it is, that your entire Being, whether perceived from the universal or from the specific standpoint, *is* this unobstructed Universe. Yes, it is the fact that You *are* this indivisible, omniactive, free, unobstructed Activity in, through, and *as* every aspect of your Body.

I would like to make two recommendations. First, it will be helpful if you will reread the previous four paragraphs. Then, it certainly will be most enlightening if you will now reread this entire chapter. In this way, Truths that may have seemed obscure, because of the necessary terminology, will be very clear indeed.

You realize, of course, that it is not easy to speak of the Body of Light in terms of a world of assumptive man-made words. Nonetheless, Beloved, here it is presented as it has been revealed. I can only speak it as it reveals itself. One thing I know — that which is herein revealed is Absolute Truth, and *You are this Truth*. Yes, this boundless, indivisible, omnipotent, omniactive Universe *is* the I AM that You are, and You are the I AM that *is* this boundless, indivisible, omnipotent, omniactive, unobstructed universal *I*.

Where am I? Wherever there is Life — and Life is everywhere — there am I, for I *am* Life. Wherever there is Spirit, Consciousness — and Spirit, Consciousness is everywhere — there am I, for I am Spirit, Consciousness. Wherever there is Mind — and Mind is everywhere — there am I, for I am Mind. Wherever there is Love — and Love is everywhere — there am I, for I am Love. Boundless, eternal, infinite, living, loving Consciousness is the entire Substance that is this Universe. I am that. That is I.

I am Life being alive; *I am Life being*. I am Consciousness being conscious; *I am Consciousness being*. I am Light, being alight; I am Light being. I am Mind being intelligent; I am Mind being. I am Love being loving; I am Love being.

I am Vision seeing; I am Vision being. I am Hearing hearing; I am Hearing being. I am Omniaction being

141

omniactive; I am Omniaction being. I am Breath breathing; I am Breath being.

I am Eternity being eternal; I am Eternity being. I am Infinity being infinite; I am Infinity being. I am Perfection being perfect; I am Perfection being. I am Completeness being complete; I am Completeness being.

I am Joy being joyous; I am Joy being. I am Order being orderly; I am Order being. I am Beauty being beautiful; I am Beauty being. I am Peace being at peace; I am Peace being. I am Immutability being immutable; I am Immutability being.

I am All being All. I am All being.

Chapter XIX

The Evidence

Sometimes it seems that our consciousness of some Truth is very clear. Yet the *manifestation* of this Truth we are so clearly perceiving is not apparent. Right here is where we should be very alert. We are inclined to question somewhat in the following manner: "Why is it that the evidence of the Truth I see so well is not apparent?" Or "What exists in my consciousness that is blocking the evidence from appearing? Isn't my understanding sufficient to meet this situation? Wherein have I failed? What Truth is it that I have failed to see?"

The foregoing questions, and many others of the same nature, will seem so persistent that, before we are aware of it, we are actually *denying* the evidence we hope to perceive. Every one of these questions is an *assumption* that the evidence of the Truth we are perceiving is not present now and here.

But this is not all. Questions such as the foregoing infer that although the evidence we are seeking is not apparent here and now, it may appear if our understanding is great enough. In this way, we would, if it were possible, delay the very evidence we wish so much to see and experience. In this way, it seems that we accept that illusion called time.

Let us perceive the glorious Absolute Fact that, actually, the evidence of any and every Truth is already present in and as our Consciousness before we even seemed to be presented with a problem. Let us pursue this aspect of Truth and the forever Fact that Truth is always Its own evidence of Itself.

You realize, of course, that duality is always the basis of any apparent failure or delay in your perception and manifestation of the Truth. When you seem to look forward to the evidence, it seems that there is an apparent separation in time between the seeing and the manifestation of the seeing.

But there is another aspect of duality to consider here. There appears to be a separation between the consciousness of this Truth and Its evidence. Why should this be? It seems to be because, to us, it is not uncommon to consider consciousness as Something and the manifestation of Consciousness as something else that is to follow or to appear. We must dispense forever with that little word *and* in all of our contemplation of Truth. Never is it Consciousness *and* Its manifestation. Always it is consciousness *being* Its manifestation, or evidence, of Itself.

The Consciousness that you are *is* the very Essence and Activity of any and every Truth that you contemplate.

> Consciousness really is Substance. Consciousness in contemplation is Substance in action. The Substance that is in action is the evidence of the Truth that you perceive.

There can be no such thing as Consciousness *and* the Truth, for Consciousness *is all Truth*. Neither can there be Consciousness, Truth, *and* evidence. Consciousness, Truth, Evidence, are *one inseparable One*. Consciousness, contemplating any Truth, is simply Consciousness aware of *being* the Substance that is that Truth It is contemplating. Contemplation is Consciousness in action. Consciousness in action is the Substance that is the Evidence, or Truth, It is contemplating.

Let us consider the way in which this Absolute Truth manifests Itself. For instance, so often we say, "I am conscious of the Truth." Or we may say, "I am knowing the Truth." To be conscious *of* the Truth may very well mean that to us the Truth we are conscious of is something separate from, or other than, the Consciousness that we are. Often we seem to know the Truth as though It were something other than the Mind we are. Right here, there does seem to be a sense of duality.

Suppose, for instance, in answer to a call for help, you are contemplating the Truth that is eternal Life. You are conscious *of* Life because you are conscious *as* Life being conscious. Life is Truth. You are conscious of the Truth that is Life. But the *only* Life there is, is eternal Life. So you are conscious as that aspect of your Self that is eternal Life.

Now, your consciousness of eternal Life is not your awareness of this Truth *and* eternal Life. Rather, it is your Consciousness as the very manifestation of this Truth. In short, your very Consciousness *as* eternal Life is the very evidence—manifestation—*of* Life that is eternal. That illusion called death can never even seem to be evidenced when you perceive clearly the foregoing Truth.

It could be that you are contemplating that aspect of Truth that is Substance. You are conscious of Substance because you are the very Consciousness that *is* Substance. In your contemplation, you perceive that aspect of Truth which is Perfection, for all Substance *is* perfect Consciousness. The very Mind, Consciousness, that you *are*, contemplating the Perfection that is Substance—the Substance that is Perfection—is the manifestation of the perfect Substance you are contemplating.

Consciousness is simultaneous with Its activity, or contemplation. There is a tremendous Truth to be realized here. This is true because enlightened perception of the foregoing statement means the instant manifestation of the Truth that you are contemplating. There is no duality here.

The manifestation of this Truth cannot now be something that follows, or comes after, your Consciousness of this aspect of Truth. Rather, your Consciousness *being* this Truth, active in contemplation *of* this Truth, is the present manifestation of the Substance that is perfect—the Perfection that is Substance.

Let us have one more example of this aspect of our contemplation. Suppose you are conscious of that Truth which is Vision. Again, you are conscious *as* the complete Truth that is perfect Vision. Your Consciousness of—or as—perfect Vision is not separate from the evidence that *is* perfect Vision. It is not your contemplation of this Truth *and* the manifestation of perfect Vision. Rather, you, conscious of the Truth that is perfect Vision, *are* the very evidence of the Truth that is perfect Vision. In short, the Consciousness that you are, aware of being the Truth you are "seeing," *is* the Substance and the Activity—the Evidence Itself.

Now you can see why it is impossible for the Evidence of any Truth you contemplate to be delayed, and you can also perceive why it is inevitable that the evidence be simultaneous with the contemplation.

Those of you who are responding to calls for help may wonder just how this way of contemplation can be helpful when those who are calling you are not present. Here again, it is well to be alert to the illusion of duality. If it appears to you that you are separate from, or other than, the Consciousness of one who has appealed for help, this sense of separation is dualism. *Consciousness is never divided.* You are not trying to know some Truth for or about someone who is a separate Consciousness from the conscious Identity that you are. Thus, you do not try to "reach" his Consciousness. Actually, your very first awareness is the fact that the Consciousness that you are is the same indivisible Consciousness that he is. But you don't stop with this perception. You also perceive that the Consciousness that he is, is the very same indivisible Consciousness that you are.

In this way, your perception of *Oneness* is complete. You know that you are Consciousness everywhere but that he also is Consciousness everywhere. It follows naturally that whatever Truth you are perceiving he also is perceiving. Right here, the precious Truth—Love—is important. Love is your Oneness. Love is his Oneness. Love is your Consciousness of being the I AM that he is. Love is his Consciousness of being the I AM that you are. Never can there be duality in Love.

Ofttimes you will find that just your awareness of being the Truth you are perceiving is so clear and so powerful that the so-called patient will instantaneously manifest the Perfection that you have perceived. In this case, you will not be actively aware of the specific Identity. But you can be assured that the universal, indivisible, omnipresent Consciousness that you are has fulfilled Its purpose *as* the Consciousness of his specific Identity. This is the meaning of the wonderful statement we find in our Bible:

> And it shall come to pass, that before they call, I will answer, and while they are yet speaking, I will hear (Isa. 65:24).

Beloved, who is it that calls? Who or what is the *I* that answers? It is the I AM who calls. It is the I AM who answers. The Consciousness that answers is the same identical Consciousness that calls.

Does a call for help really mean that the one who calls is ill or in trouble? For that matter, is it really a call for help? No! No! No! You may wonder, then, why anyone should call and ask for help.

Let us consider this last question for a moment. But first, let us realize that to believe that anyone is in need of help indicates that it appears that God is not All. All is then not God!

We know that the word *God* means Everything— *All there is, All there has ever been, All there will ever be.* It means the total, entire, indivisible, boundless Omnipresence. It means all the Life that is alive, all the Mind that is intelligent, all the Consciousness that is conscious, all the Love that loves.

Now, with this wonderful word, *God,* and all that It means in and *as* Consciousness, let us discuss just what a call for help really means. Oh, yes, the meaning remains the same, even if it is your own call for help to your own Self, *as* your Self.

God being All, All being God, there can never be any awareness of a need for help. An apparent call for help simply means that the Omnipresent All that is God is signifying His Presence right at that focal point:

> For in him dwelleth all the fulness of the Godhead bodily. And ye are complete in him, which is the head of all principality and power (Col. 2:9-10).

The Completeness that is the boundless, Universal All—the I AM that You are—does signify Its presence by evidencing Itself as All that It is at every focal point of Itself. So often, we have stated that all Substance exists in and *as* Form. The "fulness of the Godhead bodily" signifies the fact that we have just stated, namely: *All that exists as the Universe—the I AM that you are—exists as Its own evidence of Itself in, through, and as every focal point, Identity, Activity, Form, or whatever.*

In the book *You Are the Splendor,* we find an explanation of exactly what takes place when apparent trouble or evil appears. If you will read from the fourth line on page 160 in this book, and continue through the ninth line of page 161, you will remind yourself of that which is really taking place when a seeming problem appears or a call for help is received. [Editor's note: The excerpt from *You Are the Splendor* is included at the end of this chapter for the reader's convenience.]

Above all, it is well to consider the fact that *All that God is, you are.* All that you are—and all that you are as omnipresent Substance in Form, Activity, equally everywhere, constantly, and eternally—is all that God is. Wherever there is Substance, there is the "fulness of the Godhead bodily" that you are. Wherever there is Form, there is the Substance in Form that you are. Wherever there is Activity, there is the Activity that you are. There is Substance, Form, Activity, everywhere, for Substance, Form, Activity, is *the* Everywhere, and that is you—but you are also That.

This, Beloved, is why there is no "other." This is why there is no "there." This is why no call for help can come *to* you *from* anyone or anywhere outside of, or other than, your own infinite, omnipresent Allness.

The "fulness of the Godhead bodily" means that all you are universally, you are as the Entirety of this Body right here and now. It means that all that God—the I AM that You infinitely are—*is*, is present in all Completeness as the Body of everyone and everything. Form is Body. Indeed:

> You, I, everyone, everything are complete as the Universal All. The Universal All is complete as All that You are, that I am, that everyone is.

This is the Power of your "seeing." This is why the evidence of the Truth you are contemplating is inevitable. This is why you can speak as such great power. This is why you are reading these words. This is why your Heart sings as you read and contemplate the Truths herein revealed. Indeed, *You are every Truth that is revealed—eternally, infinitely, constantly.*

The inseparable *I* that you are, the *I* that I am, the *I* that everyone and everything is, exists as the *evidence* of the Completeness, the Entirety, the Wholeness, the Allness, that is the boundless, immeasurable Universe. If this were not true, there would be no evidence at all. If this were not true, there would be no existence. If this were not true, there would be no Life, Mind, Consciousness, or Love. If this were not true, there would be no God. The fact that you are conscious that you do exist is the *evidence* that God *is*.

You, conscious of being all that you are, really are "the substance of things hoped for, the evidence of things not seen" (Heb. 11:1). Oh, yes, you *are* the Life, the Truth, the Love, the Consciousness, the Mind, that is this boundless Infinity. And this universal Substance that you are is evident. It is seen, known, and experienced *now*. This is true because right *now* you know that you are. Right *now* you know *all that you are*. Right *now* you know all that you have ever been or will ever be. The evidence that you are is not unseen now because the you that you are shows, reveals, Itself as Its own evidence as all that It is.

Beloved, do you perceive the fact that if there were no Mind there would be no Existence? If there were no knowledge of *being*, no one, and nothing, could possibly be or exist. This is true because all Substance, all Form, all Activity, consists of conscious, active Mind knowing Itself to be what It is. If Substance in Form were not known, Substance in Form could not *be*.

All Substance in Form is eternal. The Mind that knows Substance in Form is eternal Mind. All Substance in Form is as eternal as is the conscious

Mind that knows Itself to be eternal. The Mind that knows Itself to be all Substance in Form also knows Itself to be the Form of all Substance. The Mind that knows Itself to be eternally, constantly active knows Itself to be the *only* activity of all Substance in Form. This is the I AM Mind that you are.

Eternal, conscious, omniactive Mind cannot know Itself to be a temporal substance. Neither can this eternal, constant Mind know Itself to be a temporary form. Eternal Omniaction cannot know Itself to be temporarily active in or as a form and substance that begins and ends. No Substance in Form ever comes into being. No Substance in Form ever goes out of being. No Form of any Substance comes into Existence, nor does It go out of Existence.

The Mind that knows Itself to be Perfection cannot know Itself to be an imperfect substance. The Mind that knows Itself to be Perfection cannot know Itself to be imperfect form. The Mind that knows Itself to be omniactive Perfection cannot know Itself to be imperfect activity. The Mind that knows Itself to be Light—all Knowledge—cannot know Itself to be darkness—ignorance. The Mind that knows Itself to be boundless and immeasurable cannot know Itself to be circumscribed or limited in any way. The Mind that knows Itself to be inseparably *One* cannot know Itself to be divided into sections of Itself. *This is the I AM Mind that You are.*

That which is called conception is really misconception. When misconception is transcended and true conception is perceived, there will no longer seem to be temporary bodies. True conception is Perception. Misconception is misperception. True conception—Perception—is eternal, conscious Mind perceiving that which It is. Thus, the eternal, birthless, changeless, ageless, deathless Body will be that which It actually is—the *only* Body. Substance in Form is forever immutable, forever perfect. Substance in Form is forever beautiful. This perfect, beautiful Substance in Form called the Body is inviolable and forever remains intact as that which It *is*.

Immaculate conception is pure Perception. It is the pure, absolute, eternal, conscious Mind—that You are—perceiving Itself to be the Substance, Form, and Activity that is this Body. It is the eternal, unadulterated, uncontaminated, conscious Mind— that You are—perceiving Itself to be the eternal, completely pure Body of Light.

Conception is supposed to precede birth. Birth is supposed to present the *appearance* of a new body. An appearance may appear to come into existence and to go out of existence; also, it can appear to change. An appearance can appear to be either perfect or imperfect. It can appear to be young or old. It can appear to be beautiful or ugly. No matter what an appearance may *appear* to be, it is only a temporary appearance. It comes, thus it must go. But an appearance is not Substance; it is not Form; nor is it Activity.

Anything that seems to appear and to disappear is as devoid of Substance, Form, and Activity as is the dream body we appear to have, or to see, while sleeping.

Substance is not an appearance. It is Reality, a positive Fact. Substance in Form is not an appearance. The Form of any Substance is not an appearance. It is genuine, eternal, constant. It is an eternal Fact, or Truth. The Activity of Substance in Form is not an appearance of activity. It is eternal, universal, Omniaction Itself. The Form of Substance can no more disappear than can the Substance of any Form. The Activity of any Substance in Form can no more begin, change, or end than can the Substance in Form Itself begin, change, or end.

Perfect, conscious Mind is the *only* Mind, Thus, all that can be known is perfect, conscious Mind, knowing Itself to be absolute Perfection. This is the I AM Mind that You are.

We know that only that which is known can exist, or be. So perfect, eternal, constant Substance, in and as perfect, constant Form, is the *only* Substance in Form that can exist. However, we also know that the perfect Form of all Substance in Form, as well as the perfect Activity, is the *only* Form that can exist. And it is all perfect, conscious Mind knowing Itself to be what It eternally, constantly, infinitely *is*. This is the I AM Mind that You are.

We have realized that anything that is not known cannot exist. Consequently, anything that does not exist cannot be known. Beloved, this is why you cannot know something that does not exist. You cannot know imperfection, for imperfection does not exist. You cannot know or be compelled to know such non-existents as lack, sorrow, trouble, or problems of any nature. You cannot know anything separate from, or other than, the perfect Mind, which is the perfect knowledge that You are.

Now it is clear that anything must be known in order to exist. It is likewise clear that anything must exist in order to be known. Anything that seems to be temporal does not really exist. You cannot know —or be compelled to know—anything that appears to come and appears to go.

An appearance is something that is *supposed* to appear, or that comes into existence. An appearance cannot *become* known. This is true because all that exists is everlastingly known. All Existence *is* the eternal, complete Mind, and there is nothing that is ever absent from, or unknown by or to, this Mind. It is all the Mind that is the sum total of all Existence, knowing Itself to be *All that It is.* This everlasting, complete, eternal, conscious Mind is the Substance, Form, and Activity of all that It knows Itself to be. This is the I Am Mind that You are.

If you did not know your Self to be, you would not exist. If you did not know your Self to be Substance, Form, and Activity, you would not have, or be, Substance, Form, and Activity. If you did not know that Body is, you would not have, or be, this

Body. If you did not know that Form is, you would not be, or have, Form. If you did not know that Activity is, you would not be, or have, Activity.

In like manner, if you did not exist, you could not know—or be conscious of—the fact that you exist. If there were no Substance in Form called the Body, you could not know that you have, or are, the Body. If there were no Omniaction, or Activity, you could not know your Self to be active, and you would not know that your Body was a constant Body, in constant, perfect action.

It is wonderful to be able to joyously proclaim:

> I know my Self to be; therefore, I am. I know my Self to be eternal, perfect, changeless; therefore, I am eternal, perfect, changeless, and immutable. I know my Self to be eternal Life, Mind, Consciousness, Love; thus, I am eternal Life, Mind, Consciousness, Love.
>
> I know my Self to be the eternal, perfect, immutable Substance in Form that is Body; therefore, I am eternal, immutable, perfect Substance in Form as this Body. All that I know my Self to be, I am. All that I am, I know my Self to be. *Only* that which I know my Self to be, am I. I am *only* that which I know my Self to be.
>
> I am One alone. There is not another. Everyone and Everything is the one *I* that I am. I am That which is Everyone and Everything, for I AM THAT I AM.

All there is of the Body is your Consciousness of that which Body *is*. Your Consciousness of Body is your Body, and It is the Body of everyone in existence. We have realized that there is one aspect of the infinite, boundless All that is the Body of Man. We have realized that this Body of Man is the Body of the Christ, or the Christ-Body. This same aspect of the universal All — Body — is the *only* Body that exists as the Body of Man.

> For as the body is one, and hath many members, and all the members of that one body being many, are one body; so also is Christ. For the body is not one member, but many. (1 Cor. 12:12, 14).

Yes, there really is but one Body. There is one aspect of the Infinite All that is the Body of Man. The Body of every Identity in existence is a member of this *one* Body. Only that which exists as Body can be the Body of you, of me, or of anyone. This fact is the basis of the statement that all there is of your Body is your Consciousness of what Body is.

What is your awareness — your Consciousness — of Body? It is your awareness of *being* the sum total, the aggregate, of all Truth. It is your Consciousness of being every Truth, such as Perfection, Beauty, Wholeness, and Eternality. It is your awareness of being eternal Life, Mind, Consciousness, Love. Of course, all of this is Spirit. This is the Body of Spirit, or the spiritual Body, that is so often mentioned.

It is your awareness of being eternal, perfect Omniaction. It is your Consciousness of being eternal, perfect, immutable, changeless Form. It is your awareness of being vibrant, dynamic, inexhaustible, undepletable. It is your awareness of being birthless, ageless, changeless, deathless. It is your awareness of being indestructible, imperishable.

In fact, your Body, right here and now, is your awareness of being all that you are infinitely, eternally, constantly. But you will realize that this Body right here and now is only the universal Consciousness that you are, aware of being what you are. You are not deceived. You are not conscious of being anything right here as *this* Body that you are not aware of being as your universal Body.

I am eternal, perfect, conscious, living Mind. Never did I begin to be this one and *only* Mind. Never can I end being this Mind. That which is called birth was but a supposititious dream incident in the constant eternity of the *I* that I am. But never was I a dreamer.

Now that I know what I am, now that I know all that I am, never will there even *seem* to be another dream incident. This is why I can never be born. This is why I can never die. Always I have known that I exist. Always will I know that I exist as just what I am and as nothing else. This awareness that *I am* is the Substance—yes, the *only* Substance—in Form right here and now. It is the eternal Substance as the eternal Body that is called my Body. Always it has been thus. Always it shall be thus. And I am that I AM evidenced.

In the beginning was the Word, and the Word was with God, and the Word was God (John 1:1).

Beloved, every Word of this Truth is the Word that is revealed in this verse. In the beginning—that is, eternally—was the Word, and the Word was with God because the Word was—is and will forever *be*—God.

These Truths are not revealed in the words of some inconsequential, even nonexistent, person. No. These Truths are the Word of God, revealing Itself *as* Itself.

You will recall this further statement from John:

And the Word was made flesh, and dwelt among us (John 1:14).

What is this Word that was, and *is*, visible as the One called Jesus? What is this Word that appears visibly as a speaker or an author? What is this Word that hears and reads and knows this Truth? What is this Word that is visible as any revelator of the absolute Truth?

Oh, the revelation *is* the revelator, even as the revelator *is* the revelation. Be assured that this revelation could not appear as a personal mind or as a personal body. It is completely devoid of personality. If some little so-called person should have the audacity to pretend to be the revelations which is the Word, the words would be meaningless, empty sounds.

Only God—the I Am that You are—can reveal the Truths that are God. Only God— the I Am that You are—can be the Word that is manifested as these writings, these tape recordings, these classes. Only God can be manifested as the Word, the Truth, the Christ, that You are, that I am, that Everyone is.

What is this Word that is made flesh? Who and what is this Word that appears among us? What is this Word that even appears to be—but is not—a temporary, born identity with a temporary body of matter? No doubt, those who saw and spoke with Jesus imagined that he was a temporary, born identity with a temporary body. But Jesus knew better than to be deceived. Most of those who see and speak with *you* imagine that you are a temporary, born identity with a temporary, born body. But you are not deceived.

Now, one may ask, "Is this Word appearing as a human being?" No! No! No! Nevertheless, this Word *is* here; It *is* manifested. Who, and what, is the manifestation of the Word that is with God, as the Word that *is* God? You are the Word. You are every Word of Truth that you can ever read, hear, write, or speak. You are the very Presence of the Word that is God.

> Put off thy shoes from thy feet: for the place where thou standest is holy ground (Acts 7:33).

Yes, right where you are aware of being this moment is "holy ground." You are wholly and completely God — that I AM that You are, that I am — pure Spirit, Perfection, Eternality, Infinity, revealing Itself to Itself, as Its Self. This is the I AM Self that You are. You are absolute, living, constant Perfection, revealing Itself as Its manifestation of Itself right here and now. There is but one Self for you to be. *You are not two, but one undivided, infinite One.*

If I were to suppose that I saw born human identities, with born bodies of matter, I would not be seeing the Word manifested at all. Actually, I would be seeing "nothing." If you were to imagine that you saw or heard a born human being with a body of matter, you would not be seeing the Word manifested. You would not be seeing the I AM that You are; nor would you be seeing the I AM that I am. If it *seemed* that all you could see was a person — man born "with breath in his nostrils" — you would be seeing nothing at all.

The only Self there is, is the Self that is God, evidencing Itself as just what God is. This is the Self that You are. You can perceive that, strictly speaking, there is no such thing as *your* Self. It is the Self that you *are,* rather than the Self that you have. You have to be the God-Self, for there is no other Self for you to be.

In the New Testament of our Bible, there are many references to everlasting Life. This word *everlasting* really means just what it says. It means Something that lasts forever. It means without beginning, change, or ending. It means the Life that is God, *being* this Life right here eternally, forever. This Life—that You are right here—is everlasting. This Life is the Life that endures forever and eternally. But this is not all that it means. It means that this Body that is alive right here and now is an everlasting, forever enduring Body.

The "Word made flesh" is the everlasting Body. It is eternal, living, loving, conscious Mind, evidencing the fact that It *is*. Its eternality manifests Itself as eternal Substance, eternal Form, eternal Activity. This is the Body that consists of the Word made flesh. This is the evidence of the Presence of all that God *is*, right here and now. This is the eternal Body. This is the birthless, changeless, deathless Body of Light. This is the infinite Body *being* the Body that You are. This is the infinite You being this Body.

Never did you become aware of being this Body. Never can you become unaware of being this Body. This does not mean that your attention is focused constantly as this Body; quite the contrary. But you can no more be or become completely unaware of this Body than you can become completely unaware of your Self. You see, this Body *is* You, even as You *are* this Body.

Jesus walked and talked with those about him as "the Word made flesh." This Word really was— and is—the Body of the Identity called Jesus. It was necessary for the people to see the Body of Jesus. Although it is true that they did not actually see his everlasting Body as It is, yet the body they saw was—as far as they were concerned—the evidence of the fact that Jesus was an Identity. Had his Body not appeared in a way that they could understand, they would have had no evidence of his existence. Nonetheless, Jesus knew—and knows—the eternality of his Body.

In like manner, it is necessary for those about you to be able to see something that they *imagine* to be your Body. Even this appearance of Body fulfills a certain purpose. But you are not deceived. You *know* that the everlasting Body, comprised of living, conscious, loving Mind, is *this* Body right here. You know that—even though this Body may appear to be temporal and material—this Body is eternal, indestructible, imperishable. Yet at the present, it sometimes seems necessary for this glorious Body to appear as something other than It is. Of course, as your friends occasionally see you, they will comment upon how much better or younger you are looking, but you will not be flattered or deceived by these statements. You will simply know that the Body that you genuinely *are* is evidenced, and this is as it should be.

There is nothing that can keep this Body that you have, and are, from revealing and manifesting Itself *as what It is*. Beloved, there is nothing in existence that can possibly prevent this Body that is the Word made flesh from *being* the evidence of that which It is, that which It has always been, and that which It will eternally be.

Yes, You, the Word made flesh, are God manifested, God evidenced. You know that God can only manifest Itself as God. So you, the Word made flesh, are the very evidence, the manifestation, that *is* God manifesting Itself—God evidencing Itself as what God is.

You are not a separate You. You are the manifest Presence of the Power that is God. You are the *evidence* of the Presence that is God. God is not a purposeless God. God is Mind, Intelligence, and Intelligence must have a purpose in being. God fulfills Its purpose by being the evidence of Itself. And *You are this Evidence.*

Now, let us go a step further. *What are you?* Are you not just what God is? You know that you could not even exist if you were other than God being God, yet God being all there is of You. Thus, you know that You—the very evidence of the fact that God is—are the very Presence of God, evidencing Itself as just what God is. From this fact, you can perceive the indisputable Truth that the universal You that You are really is evidenced as the You that You are right here and now.

This is what it means to be the *I* that I am. This is the true meaning of the statement "I AM THAT I AM." Even so, you will realize that only because God *is*, can you be. Yet you will also perceive the Truth that if there were no You, there would be no God. You are necessary to the manifestation of the Presence that is God. You—right here and now—are essential to the evidence of the fact that You—the boundless, immeasurable, infinite You—really *are*.

Beloved, this is what you are. This is what you have always been and will ever be. Rejoice in this Truth, and forever *be* the evidence of the fact that the boundless, infinite, universal I AM that you eternally are really is manifested.

Now that we know that there is nothing and no one but God, let us perceive and silently speak the words of the next concluding paragraphs. But let not one of us go about and say them publicly. These are words that can only be spoken in the revelation of complete selflessness.

Thus, in infinite humility and yet as Omnipotence Itself announcing Its Presence, we can say:

I AM THAT I AM. I am the Word that is with God, for I am the Word that *is* God. God is the Presence that I am. I am the Presence that is God. I am God manifested. I am the Power that is God, for I am Omnipotence manifested. I am the Life that is God, for I am Life manifested. I am the Mind that is God, for I am Mind evidenced. I am the Love that is God. I am Love evidenced right here and now. I am the Consciousness that is God. I am the God-Consciousness evidenced right here and now.

I am the boundless, living Light that is all Substance, all Form, all Activity. I am the Constancy of all Life, of all that lives, for I am Life manifested. I am the Constancy of all Form. I am the Constancy of all Substance. I am the Constancy of all Activity. I am the Constancy of all Mind. I am the

Constancy of all Consciousness. I am the Constancy of all Love, for I am the infinite Love that loves.

I am the Eternality that *is* all Life, all Mind, all Consciousness, all Love. I am the Eternality that is all Substance. I am the Eternality that is all Substance in Form. I am the Eternality of all Activity. I am the Eternality of all rhythmic tempos. I am the Constancy, the Eternality, that is all Truth.

I am the Substance, Form, and Activity of the galaxies in their ever surging, flowing, swirling movements. I am the Substance, Form, and Activity of all stars and planets, as they ceaselessly orbit in, through, and as Infinity. I am the Substance, Form, and Activity of the bird in its flight. I am the Substance, Form, and Activity of the tree, the flower, and the fresh green grass. I am the Substance, Form, and Activity of all that is called the dust of the ground. I am the Substance and Activity of the very Air Itself. I am the Substance, Form, and Activity of the oceans, the mountains, and the valleys. I am the Substance, Form, and Activity of the sands of the spaceless, timeless desert. I am the Substance, Form, and Activity of all that is, for I am *that* I AM.

I am the sum total that is all Truth. I *am* the *All that is true*. I am *only* that which is Truth. I am omnipresent Perfection. I am omniactive Perfection. I am omni-loving Perfection. I am omnipotent Perfection. I am eternal Perfection. I am the Perfection that is All. I am the All that is Perfection.

I am the Light that lighteth every Man that cometh into the world of fantasy. I am the Light that shines wherever darkness *seems* to be—and there is no darkness. I am the Heaven that is right where hell *seems* to be. I am the Joy that is where sorrow *seems* to be. I am the "peace, be still" where storms appear to rise. I am the indivisible All where separateness seems to be.

I am the Immutability of All that is. I am infinite, eternal Completeness. I am all order. I am all balance. I am the All that is perfect control. I am all government. I am the perfect, changeless, rhythmic activity of all that acts. I am all rhythms. I am All that acts. I am the Beauty of the Heavens. I am the Beauty of the Earth. I am the Beauty of song, the symphony, the painting, the poem. I am the Beauty of all that is beautiful—and All is beautiful—for I am Beauty.

I am the only Life that is alive. I am the only Consciousness that is conscious. I am the only Mind that is intelligent. I am the only Love that loves, for I am that I AM.

What is the *I* that I am? There is one *I*. There is one I AM, and there is no other. There is but one God. I must be just what this one I AM— God—is, else I could not even say, "I am." Thus, the *I* that I am—God—can, and does, say, "I am God.

Having thus spoken, I have said all there is. Having thus spoken, there is nothing more that can be said.

[Editor's note: The following excerpt is from *You Are the Splendor*, Chapter 10, pp. 160-161 (published by Mystics of the World) to which the author referred on page 150 of this chapter.]

If apparent evil serves to draw your attention to God, or Good, then apparent evil is not evil, but good. It is God—who comprises your entire Existence—revealing Its Omnipresence. It makes no difference what the specific appearance of evil may be; the specific fact is already established in and as your own Consciousness. Your attention is simply being called to the specific fact. Thus, any appearance of evil must be but a signal signifying the presence of God, Good, Perfection. Now you perceive the truth of the statement, "There is no evil." You also realize why this statement is true.

The appearance of a material universe signifies the presence of the Universe of Light, or Spirit. The appearance of solidity signifies the presence of the Essence which is spiritual. An appearance of density, or darkness, signifies the presence of Light. The appearance of stupidity signifies the presence of Intelligence. In like manner, any appearance of temporal life, mind, consciousness signifies the presence of eternal Life, Intelligence, Consciousness.

The appearance of a personal "I"—assumptive man—signifies the presence of God evidencing Itself as the Identity. The assumptive "born body" signifies the eternal Body, comprised of Life, Mind, Consciousness. The assumption that there is a human mind centered in a brain signifies the presence of infinite Intelligence, specifically identified. The appearance of a human consciousness, or life, is the signal announcing the presence of the infinite, eternal, conscious Life, identified as the specific conscious Life. That which is called human activity signifies the infinite Universe in action, or Omniaction, identified as specific activity. Our task is to keep the attention centered upon the universal, as well as the specific, Existence which is being signified.

[End of Excerpt]

The *I* That I Am

The I that I am is evident
As All there is of me;
The I that I am is omnipotent
Love only can I be.

I soar as the bird in its joyous flight
in ecstasy sublime;
I know that I am the living Light
beyond all space or time.

The I that I am is ever blest
as constant perfect "seeing;"
The All that I am dost manifest
as omnipresent Being.

The Life that I am is eternally,
inseparably the same;
The All that I am is Infinity,
for I AM is my Name.

About the Author

During early childhood, Marie S. Watts began questioning: "Why am I? What am I? Where is God? What is God?"

After experiencing her first illumination at seven years of age, her hunger for the answers to these questions became intensified. Although she became a concert pianist, her search for the answers continued, leading her to study all religions, including those of the East.

Finally, ill and unsatisfied, she gave up her profession of music, discarded all books of ancient and modern religions, kept only the Bible, and went into virtual seclusion from the world for some eight years. It was out of the revelations and illuminations she experienced during those years, revelations that were sometimes the very opposite of what she had hitherto believed, that her own healing was realized.

During all the previous years, she had been active in helping others. After 1957, she devoted herself exclusively to the continuance of this healing work and to lecturing and teaching. Revelations continually came to her, and these have been set forth in this and every book.

To all seekers for Truth, for God, for an understanding of their own true Being, the words in her books will speak to your soul.

64618349R10106

Made in the USA
Charleston, SC
03 December 2016